BROADS-MANSHIP

Richard Simpkin

a guide to safe boating on the norfolk broads

Cartoons by Nicholas Walmsley

Illustrations by Chas Emerson

Published in association with Bayard Books

BARRIE & JENKINS
COMMUNICA-EUROPA

First published in Britain in 1976

ISBN 0 214 20285 2

This book has been set 10pt IBM Univers Medium, prepared for press by The Ivory Head Press, 170 Murray Road, London W5, and printed in England by Richard Clay (The Chaucer Press) Limited, Bungay, Suffolk, for the publishers, Barrie & Jenkins Limited
Publishing office: 24 Highbury Crescent, London N5 1RX

Foreword

Every year about one million people use boats on the Broadland Rivers, in addition to a large number who enjoy being on the banks. The Rivers Yare, Bure and Waveney Commissioners hope that everyone will enjoy themselves as much as possible but it is important that one person's enjoyment is not spoilt by another person's behaviour. The Commissioners therefore commend this book and hope that all who read it will follow the rules of navigation thus enabling more people to enjoy themselves. Correct handling of a boat will add to the enjoyment and prevent damage or injury.

A. D. TRUMAN
Chairman of the Rivers Yare, Bure and Waveney Commissioners.

Contents

Introduction

For most of the time steering a ship or piloting an aircraft is considerably easier than driving a car in average traffic. But because water and air are not the elements that man usually moves through, unusual situations or crises can arise quickly and call for a speedy and skilled response. That is one reason why ships' masters and aircraft pilots undergo years of training and experience before they are given command. The other reason is that training and experience makes these professionals able to foresee difficulties and steer clear of them or nip them in the bud.

Handling a modern powerboat on inland waters is by and large a very safe and simple business; but problems can and do arise, and accidents do happen.

This book sets out in simple easily understood terms what the special features of travelling by water as opposed to land are, and how to avoid problems or if needs be deal with them – what the amateur skipper needs to know to go where he wants safely and to keep out of trouble. A few minutes spent looking through it will make your own and your crew's holiday more interesting, relaxed and enjoyable. By doing things the right way, you can take a pride in your skill and save your crew a lot of hard work and stress.

AND MAYBE SAVE YOU OR ONE OF YOUR FAMILY FROM A SERIOUS, EVEN FATAL ACCIDENT.

Explanation of symbols

To save a lot of words and complicated instructions, the following symbols are used throughout this book.

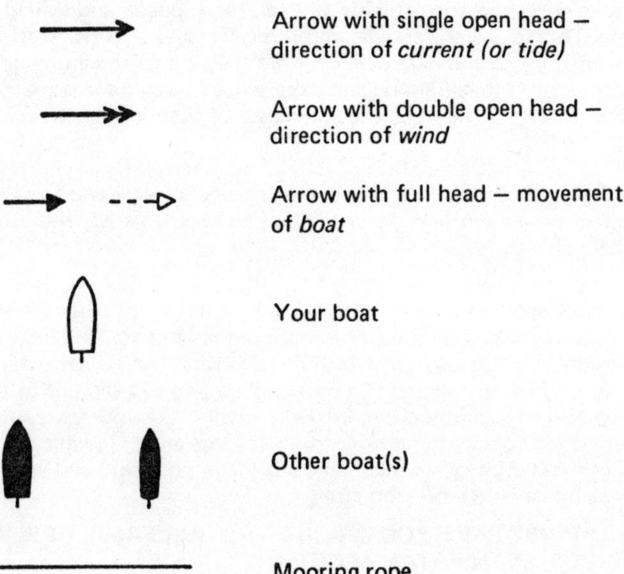

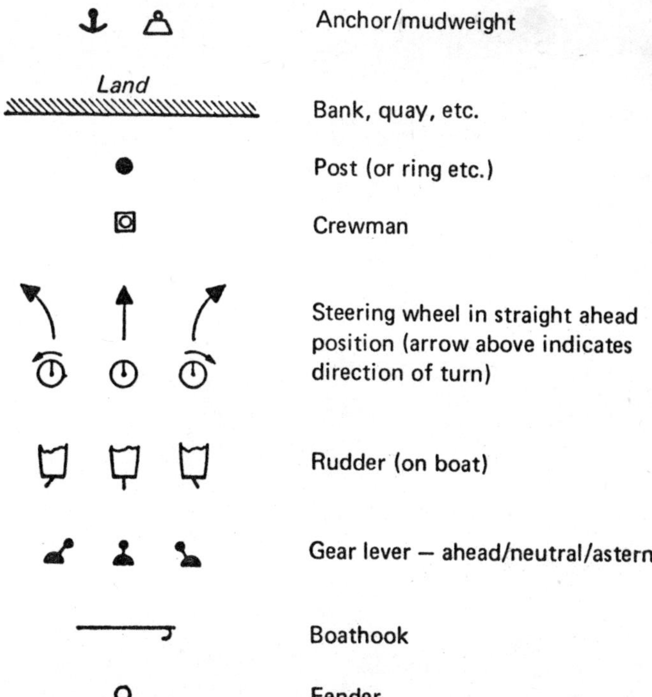
Anchor/mudweight
Land
Bank, quay, etc.
Post (or ring etc.)
Crewman
Steering wheel in straight ahead position (arrow above indicates direction of turn)
Rudder (on boat)
Gear lever – ahead/neutral/astern
Boathook
Fender

Glossary

You can operate a powerboat well without knowing the jargon with which sailors love to puzzle and impress; but a little of it does help!

BOW	The front of a boat, i.e. the end which goes first when the boat is moving in its normal direction of travel.
STERN	The other end.
PORT (SIDE)	The side on your *left* as you look from within the boat towards the bow.
STARBOARD (SIDE)	The side on your *right* as you look from within the boat towards the bow.
AHEAD	The normal direction of travel. 'Going ahead' = moving forwards
ASTERN	The opposite to *ahead.* 'Going astern' = moving backwards. Unlike a car, a boat may still be moving forwards (ahead) when it is in reverse gear ('going astern') – and vice versa. Reverse gear is used as a brake.

MOORING	Securing the boat by rope(s) to the bank or some other fixed object.
ANCHORING	Securing the boat by means of an anchor or mudweight resting on the bottom.
BUOYANCY AID	A safety garment which, *if properly worn,* will safely support a person in the water provided that he is conscious and can turn on his back.
LIFEJACKET	A low-density or inflatable safety garment which, *if properly worn,* will turn an unconscious or incapacitated person onto his back and then support him safely in the water.
LIFEBELT	A buoyant ring or horseshoe which can be thrown to a person in the water to support them and to make them more easily visible.

Knots

Like jargon, knots, whips and splices are great mysteries of the sea, but you need to know only a very few of them. But quick use of the right knot can save a great deal of inconvenience and *maybe even save a life.*

Ends of synthetic ropes

If you have to cut a nylon or terylene rope, *fuse the ends immediately* with a cigarette-lighter flame or a match. Take the obvious fire precautions and avoid getting burnt by the hot ends or by drips or pieces falling from the rope. In an *emergency* you can stop a cut or broken rope unravelling by *tying a knot (half-hitch) in the end.*

Useful knots

1 Taking a turn

Simply pass the end of the rope round the piece of wood or whatever, or loop the rope over the end of the wood. This is not secure, but will take the pull as long as the spare end is held.

2 Reef knot

This is a knot normally used to join two ropes of roughly equal size. It is one form of the 'double knot' used in everyday life. The usual way to remember it is 'left over right, right over left', but it may be easier to remember that you do all the tying with the same end (the 'left' becoming the 'right' after the first half-hitch is tied).

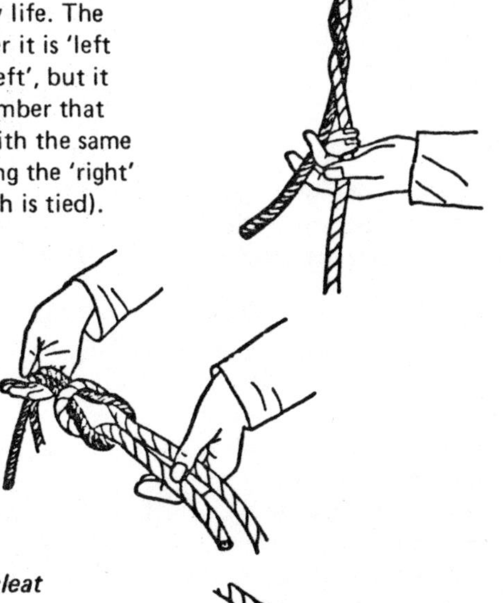

3 Securing rope to cleat (jamming hitch)

Go round once.

Cross over once.

Cross over again and form loop with slack end under.

Hoop loop over cleat and pull tight on slack end.

Note: Don't use this hitch for the halliards of dinghy sails or sailing dinghy centreboards – see a book on sailing.

4 Clove hitch

This is used for securing a mooring rope to a post when either the top of the post or the end of the rope is accessible.

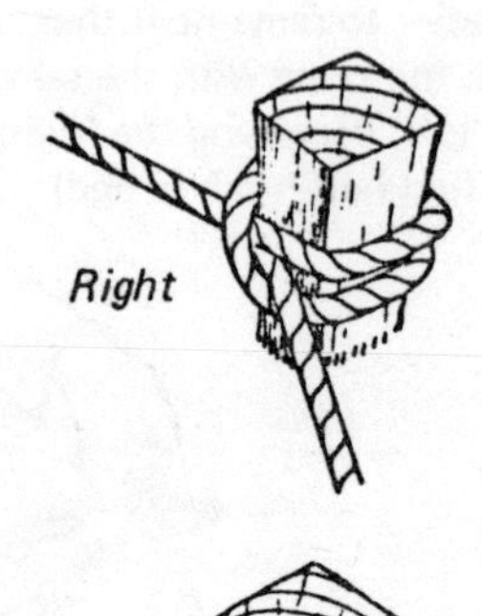

Right

It is very simple to tie, but also very easy to get wrong by doubling the second turn back. It is normally done right-handed (clockwise), but goes equally well the other way. Using this knot it is very easy to adjust the length of rope between boat and post.

Wrong

OVER TOP OF POST

1 Make a loop with the slack end passing *under* the run of the rope.

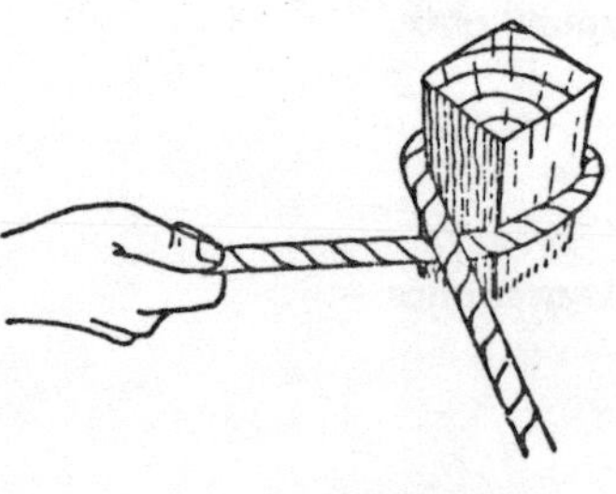

2 Drop loop over post.

3 Repeat, *continuing in the same direction.*

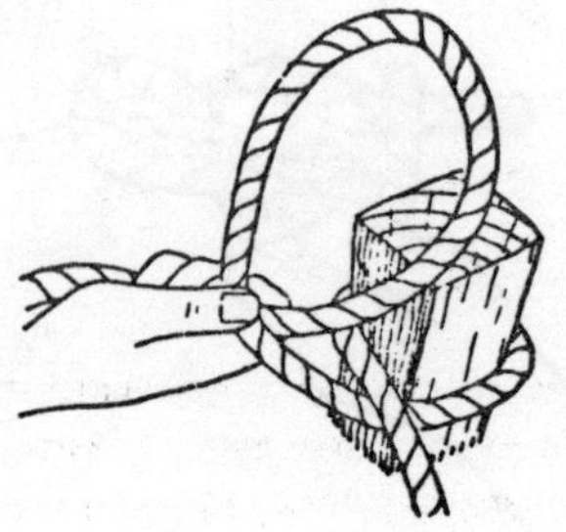

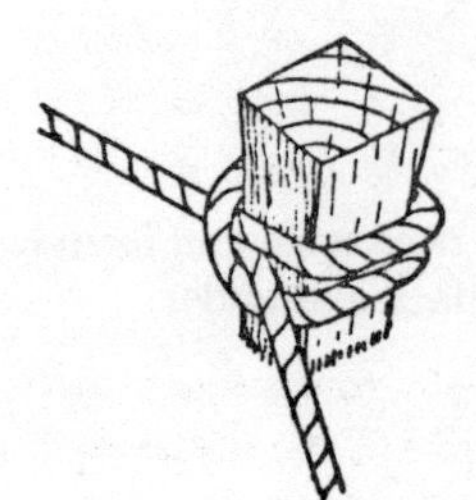

USING END OF ROPE

1 Pass slack end round post and *under* run of rope.

2 *Continue in same direction,* passing slack end *over* run of rope and first turn.

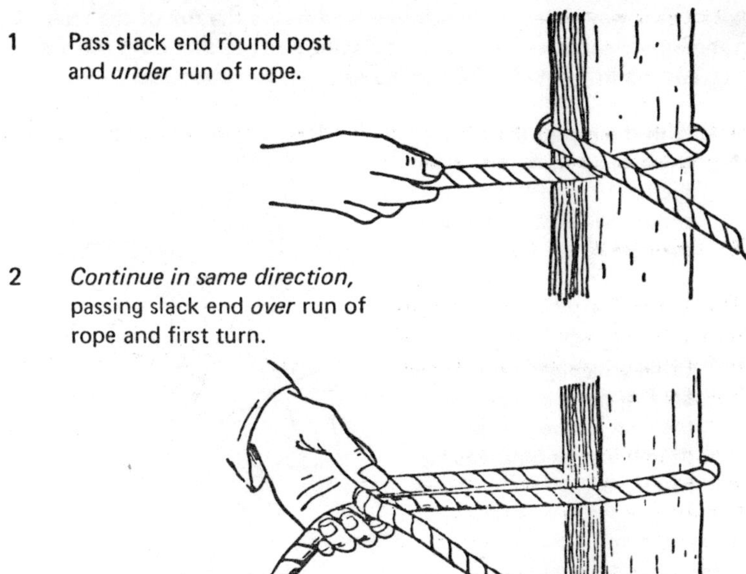

3 *Continue in same direction,* passing slack end *under* second turn.

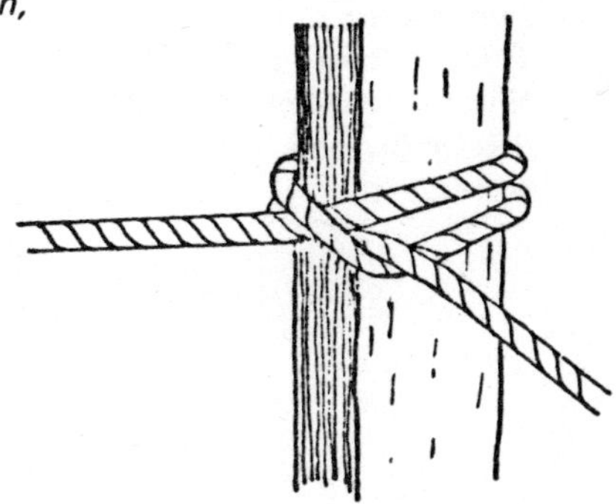

5 Bowline

Sailors, climbers and others whose lives depend on ropes regard the bowline as the lifesaving knot. It is not particularly easy to learn, but it is secure, easy to undo and will serve any purpose requiring a loop in the end of a rope, including tying a rope to a ring.

The easy way to learn the bowline is to secure the run of the rope to something and pass the rope round your waist so that both run and slack end are in front of you. *Leave a long enough spare end.*

1 With the run of the rope going away from you, take the run in your left hand at about the point you want the base of the loop to be.

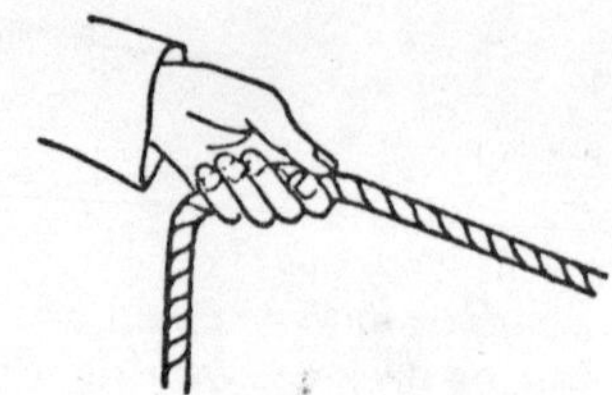

2 Bring your right hand across *back of hand up* and grasp the rope between finger and thumb just beyond your left hand.

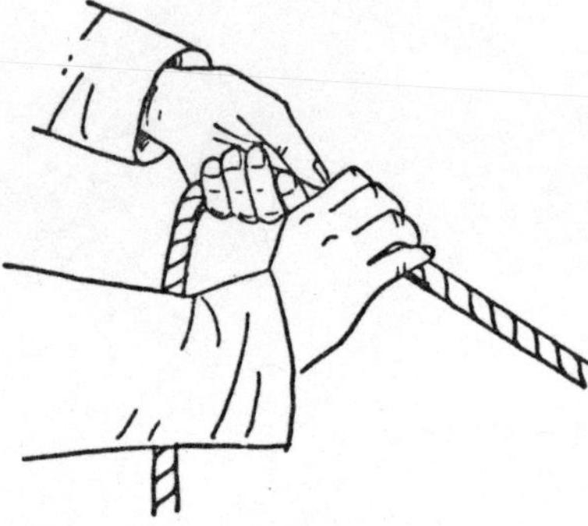

3 Turn your right hand *away from you till it is palm up.* This will form a small loop with the run *under* the slack. Secure this loop with your left thumb.

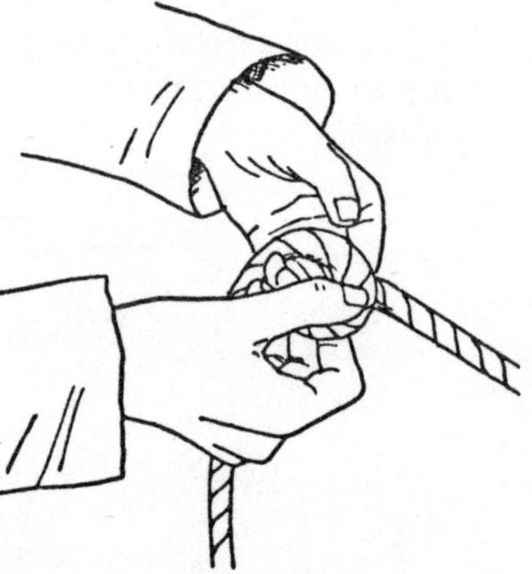

4 Take the slack with your right hand and pass it *up* through the loop, *round* the run and *back down* through the loop. 'The rabbit comes out of the hole, round the tree and down into its hole again.'

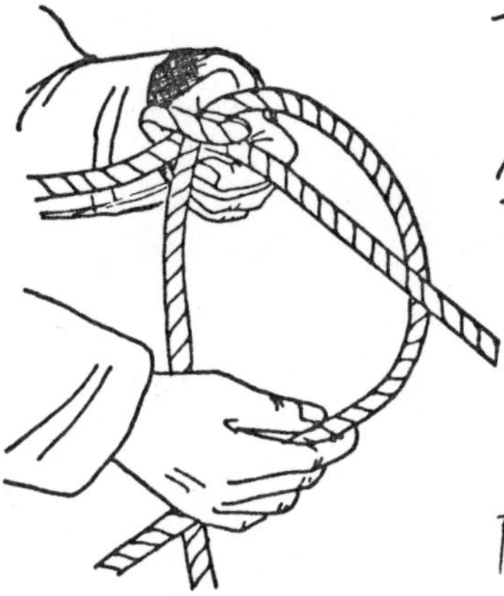

5 Tighten as shown, leaving enough spare end.

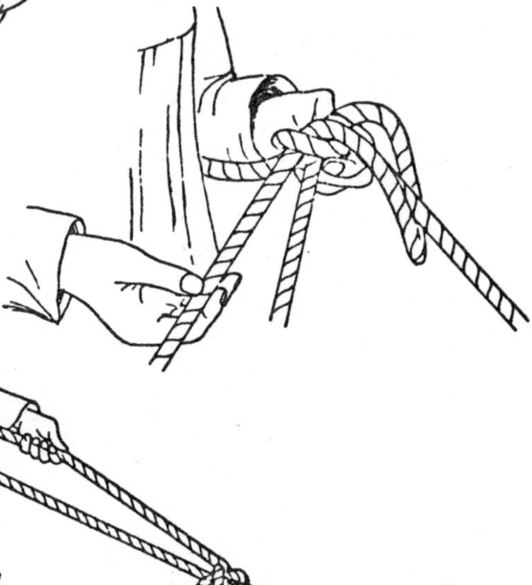

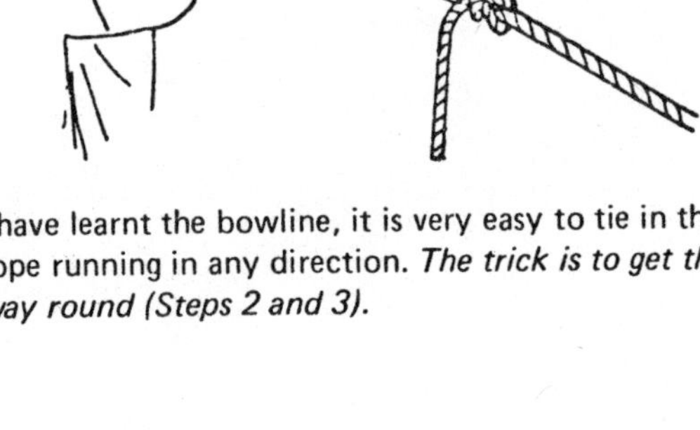

Once you have learnt the bowline, it is very easy to tie in the dark and with the rope running in any direction. *The trick is to get the small loop the right way round (Steps 2 and 3).*

1 The Broads

The Norfolk Broads are a system of shallow lakes (mainly old peat diggings), rivers and canals (called 'dykes'). The whole system is open to the sea, having no locks or barrages except between Oulton Broad and Lowestoft Harbour.

To find your way on the Broads, you need a cruising map. If you want to explore thoroughly, a navigation index (which includes maps/charts) may be helpful, but most cruising maps of the Broads include some navigational information, e.g. depths and state of banks. To plan your passage through Great Yarmouth you will need to know *the time of low water at Yarmouth Yacht Station.* Tables giving this are available – ring Yarmouth Yacht Station (Great Yarmouth 2794) or ask at a boatyard. Don't try to work it out from ordinary sea tide tables which give high water at Yarmouth Bar (see below).

Tides

Heavy rain and strong winds in certain directions may affect both the pattern of currents and the level of water, but normally the navigable waters are all *tidal*. This means that when the tide comes in (twice every 24 hours) the current flows inland from the sea and the water level rises; when the tide goes out the water flows towards the sea and the level falls.

Tide-wise you can think of the Broads as being divided into three zones (see sketch-map).

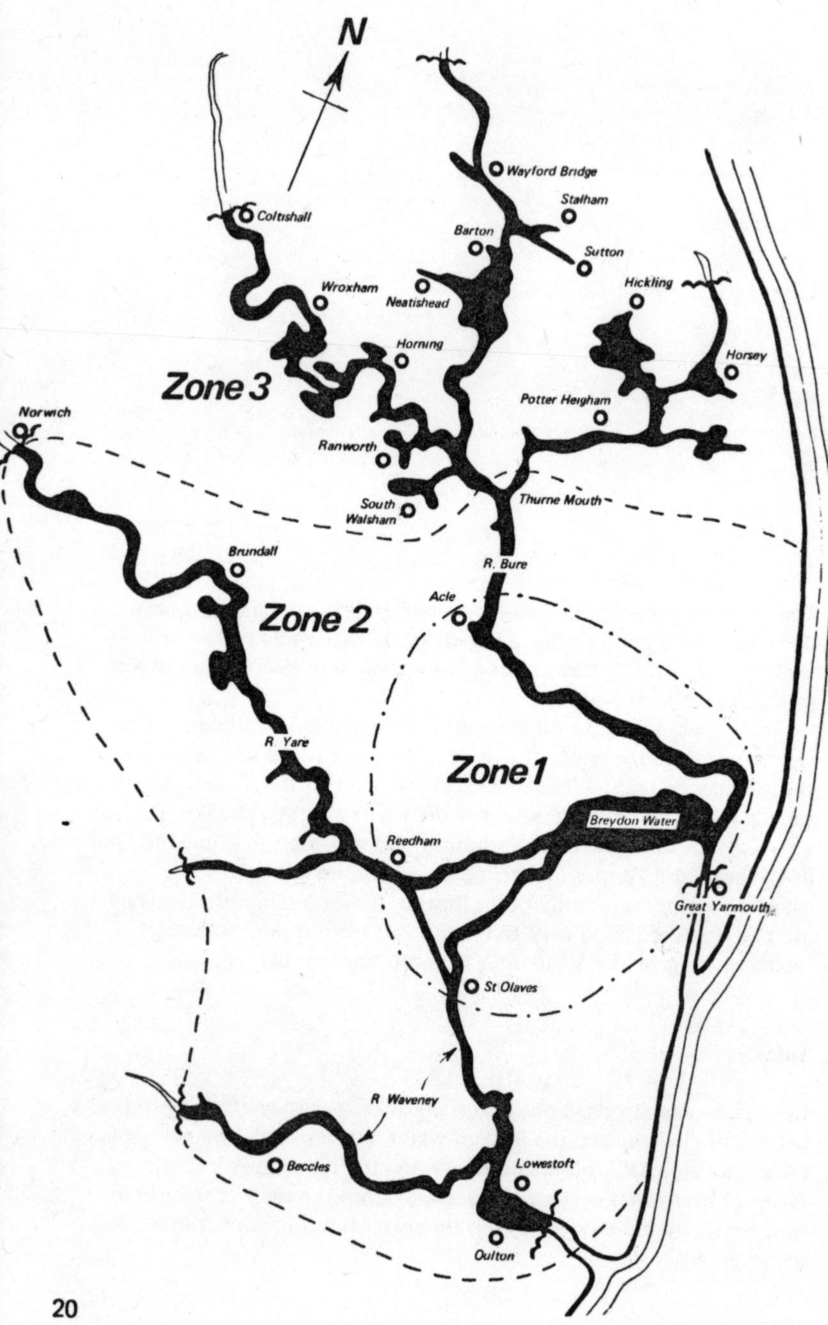

1 Between Great Yarmouth and Acle (River Bure), Reedham (River Yare and St Olaves (River Waveney)

In this zone you will need to take the tide seriously. The rise and fall may be 6 to 10 feet with currents running at up to 6 miles per hour.

Plan your passage to make use of the tides. The safest time to pass through Great Yarmouth is at *low water slack at Yarmouth Yacht Station*. Oddly enough this is 1¼ hours after low water at Yarmouth Yacht Station (and about 2¼ hours after low water at Yarmouth Bar). Motor cruisers of normal power can safely navigate the lower Bure (provided they can clear the bridges) and Breydon Water for 2-3 hours either side of the slack water time, especially when the tides are small ('neaps'). But when the tides are running strongly the narrow crowded channel that forms the last mile of the River Bure can produce alarming and sometimes genuinely dangerous situations.

Watch crosswinds on Breydon Water; they tend to blow you out of the channel.

Don't moor in this zone except at regular moorings, which are at:

Bure	Stokesby, Stacey Arms, Yarmouth Marina, Yarmouth Yacht Station
Yare	Berney Arms
Waveney	Burgh Castle

If you do not moor at these places, you may find that the tide has taken the water from under you and left you aground on the edge of a mudbank. This is uncomfortable *and very dangerous.*

Even on a regular mooring, *test the depth with your boathook and leave enough slack* on your mooring rope to allow for the fall of the tide (see above) when you leave the boat or before you go to sleep. Otherwise you may find the boat hanging on its ropes and all ready to turn over and decant you and yours into the channel.

NAVIGATING YARMOUTH

(views depicted as at half tide)

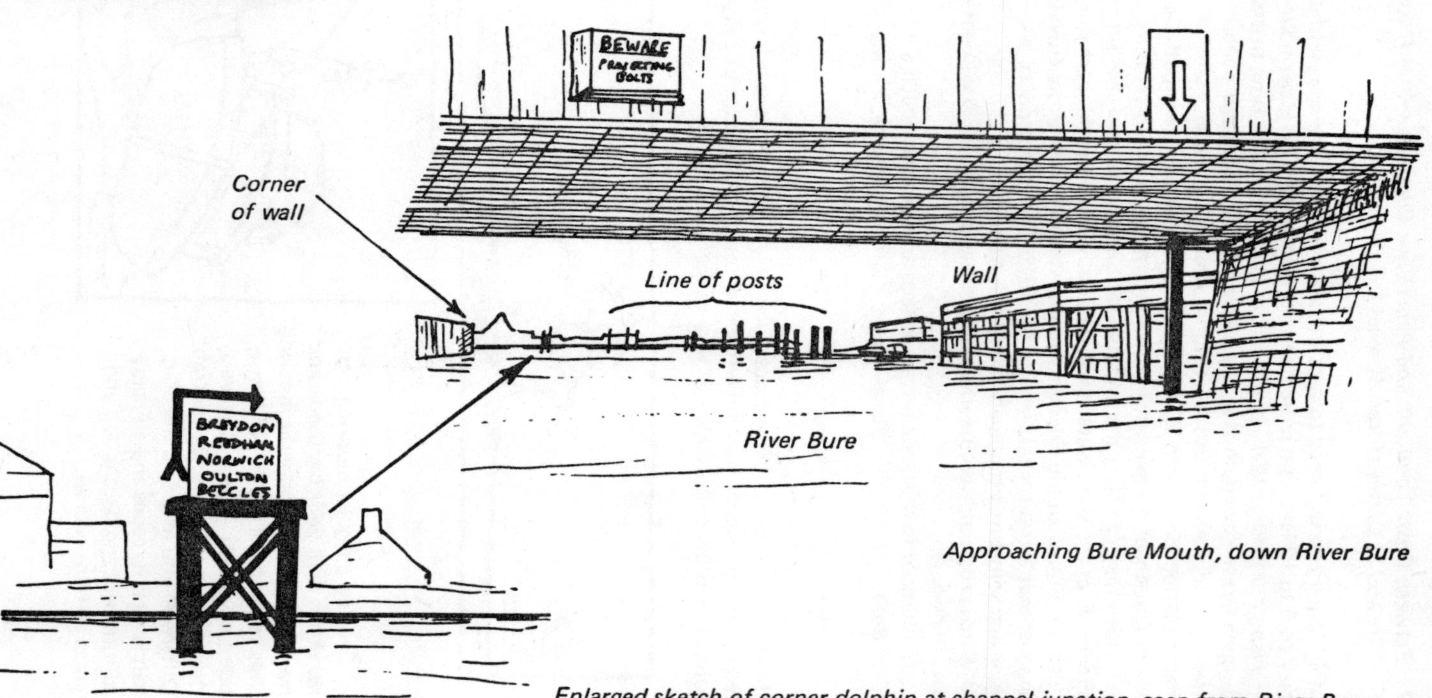

Approaching Bure Mouth, down River Bure

Enlarged sketch of corner dolphin at channel junction, seen from River Bure

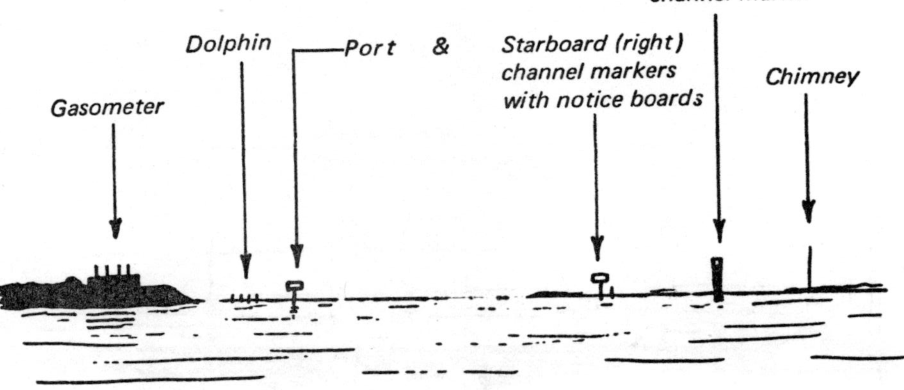

Entry to Breydon Water from Yare/Bure junction

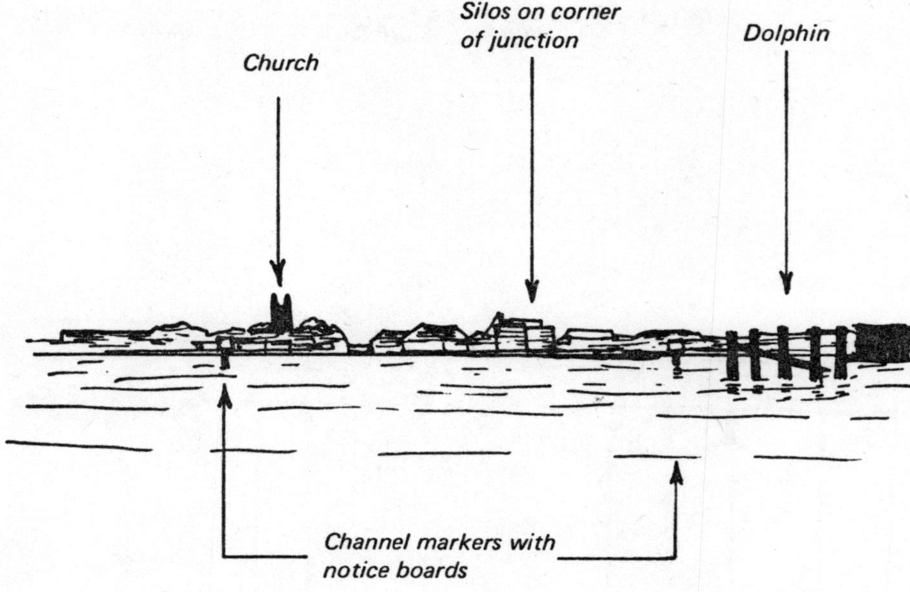

Approaching Yare/Bure junction (Bure Mouth) from Breydon Water

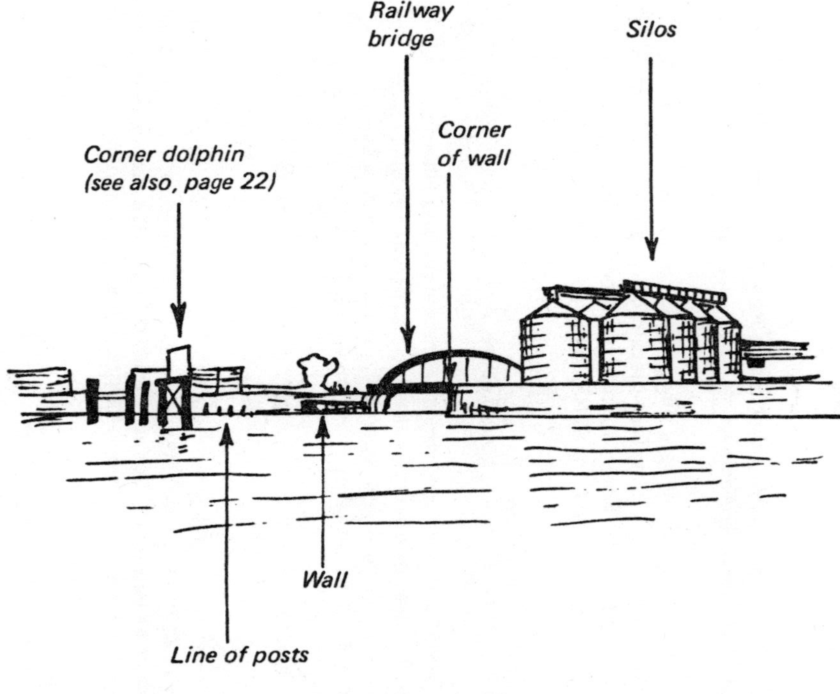

Entry to River Bure seen from south side of channel at junction

In this zone, DON'T LET ANYONE USE OR EVEN GET INTO THE DINGHY, even when you are moored up, unless you are sure that he or she can row the dinghy well enough to make good against the worst of the tide.

Don't allow children or non-swimmers on the roof or top deck, even if the boat is moored and they are wearing a buoyancy aid. The tide can sweep them away before you even know they've fallen in.

Until you know the waters well, make an 'adventure' of your passage through Great Yarmouth. Then you – and especially your children – will enjoy planning it and doing it. And you will have no problems.

2 Acle – Thurne Mouth (Bure), above Reedham (Yare and Chet), above St Olaves (Waveney)

In these stretches you will save time, stress and fuel by moving with the tide as much as you can. Take precautions as above if the tide is running very strongly. Under normal conditions you can safely moor anywhere that is free of hazards (see below).

3 Above Thurne Mouth (Bure, Thurne, Ant, broads and dykes)

Here the tides are weak and irregular and the rise and fall only 12-18 inches. Powerboats can ignore the tide except when passing under bridges or mooring. There is normally no risk of dinghies being swept away. You can safely moor anywhere that is clear of hazards.

Before we leave tides, the table below tells you how long after low water at Yarmouth Yacht Station the current stops flowing towards the sea at various points up the rivers. *To find LOW water at these places, ADD the times given to LOW water at Yarmouth Yacht Station:*

Acle	2½	Oulton Broad	3
Barton	3½	Potter Heigham	3
Beccles	3	Reedham	1½
Brundall	3	St Olaves	1½
Horning	3	Wroxham	3½
Norwich	3½		

When using any tide table, *check whether the times given are Greenwich Mean Time (GMT) or British Standard Time (BST),* and add an hour when necessary.

Hazards

On Breydon Water and some of the broads you will see marked channels. *Keep within* these channels, but *don't* anchor in them – above all *don't* moor to the channel marker posts. If you want to anchor, ease very gently *up wind* clear of the channel.

On the rivers and in the dykes there are a few places where you may run aground if you get too close to the banks but the main hazards are man-made ones.

WRECKS	are either visible or clearly marked by a RED flag and/or an appropriate channel marker buoy.
STONES, etc.	are normally marked by warning notices on the bank affected.
OLD PILING	with its tops under water, both on banks which are now natural and outside new piling, is very dangerous. Sometimes it is marked with RED flags, *but always consult your map or index before mooring.* Take particular care on the River Ant between Barton Broad and Ludham Bridge.
TREESTUMPS	underwater, may be unmarked and unmentioned as clearance is going on all the time. Keep well clear of banks where there are signs of recent tree or undergrowth clearance.
EEL NETS	are marked with RED flags and/or lights. Keep in the middle. Read and follow the instructions on the notice boards you will see as you approach.
TEMPORARY OBSTRUCTIONS	Dredgers, barges, workboats, etc. are normally marked by a RED flag, and a flashing light at night. Their anchor cables are usually marked by RED or YELLOW drum buoys. Whatever craft you are in, keep well clear.

If you keep reasonably clear of the banks and any obvious obstructions, you will usually be quite safe while you are on the move. But you always need to *take care when mooring,* as the tide may go out and let you down onto a wood or metal spike, or a stump, and any sharp or jagged end will make a hole in the hull.

An up-to-date navigation index is useful for choosing isolated moorings but it is no substitute for *a good probe around with the boathook as you come in and as soon as you have tied up.*

Speed limits

Many parts of the Broads have speed limits of 5 or 7 miles per hour in force. Their purpose is to reduce damage to banks and inconvenience or even danger to moored boats from the wash of powerboats. Engine speeds corresponding to these limits should be marked on the rev counter of hire boats and private owners should know these for themselves.

It is worth remembering, especially on narrow channels, that ideally you should not be going so fast that your wash is breaking on the banks (this causes bank erosion) – even though you may be doing far less than the legal limit. If, in addition, the channel is shallow, this will restrict your speed and opening up the throttle will not make you go faster – the extra engine power will be used up in overcoming increased drag.

Speed limits are also a safety measure, as the waters where they apply are sometimes narrow and often crowded with dinghies. Failure to observe them is not only against the law; it is also a mark of the kind of skipper best described as an accident about to happen.

Anglers

The wash of passing boats removes the bait from hooks and boats may foul tackle. As a matter of courtesy, slow right down when passing anglers and keep as far as possible from the bank being fished.

2 Handling your boat

Wind and current

When you park your car, you have to put the handbrake on; but you don't tie the car up. Neither car nor ground can move. When you stop your boat you have to secure it to a post or two, or anchor it to the bottom. If you don't fix it to the ground, it will go away because:

1 The water it is lying in may be moving past the ground *(current tide)* and/or

2 Movement of the air may push the boat through the water *(wind)*.

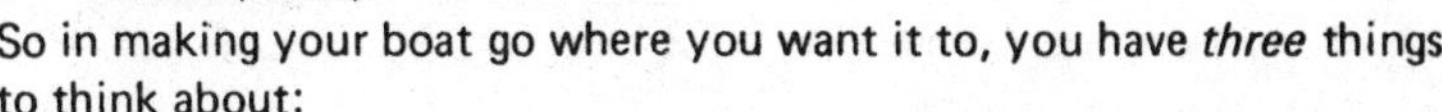

So in making your boat go where you want it to, you have *three* things to think about:

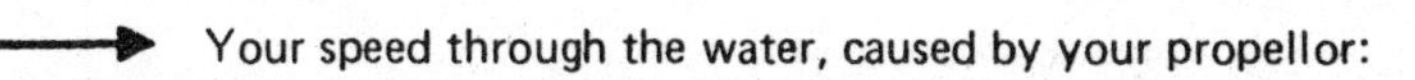

→ Your speed through the water, caused by your propellor:

→→ The wind blowing you sideways – or forwards, or backwards:

→ The water moving past the land

The first of these you can control; the other two you have to allow for. Suppose you bring your boat to rest with head to current and side to wind.

It will drift like this

Or, perhaps, more mysteriously, like this

It swings so far and then goes on drifting at the same angle. The fact that this can happen tells us a lot about the effect of wind and current on a boat.

Take a typical inland waters motor-cruiser.

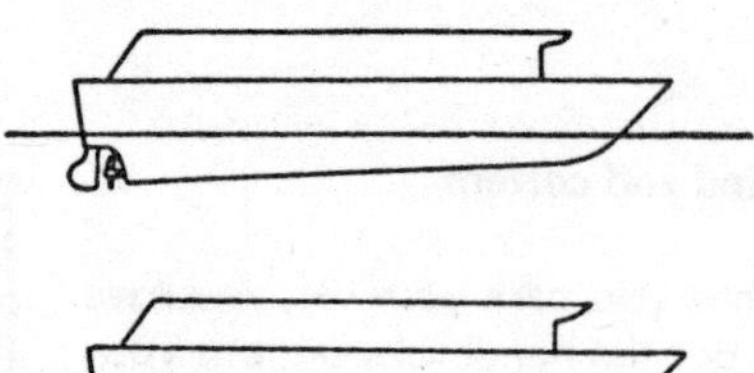

Suppose we draw a view of the right hand (starboard) side of the boat – or even better make a card-board cut-out – and then divide it in two along the waterline.

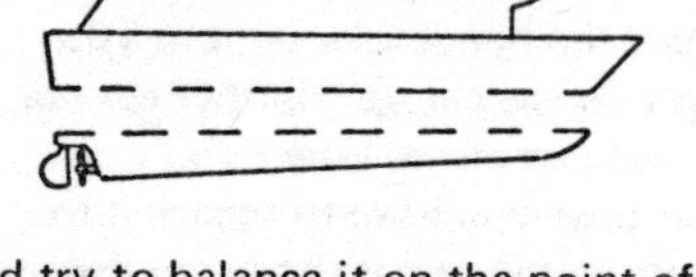

Take the top half first, turn it flat and try to balance it on the point of a pencil. By moving the pencil about under it, you will find a point at which it balances. This we can think of as the 'middle', although it may not be exactly half-way between one edge and the other. Mark it with a double ring (to match the double arrowhead for wind).

Now turn this top part upright again and think of the wind blow-on it. Clearly it will push the boat sideways. The wind of course blows on the whole surface, but we can think of it as *pushing at the middle,* like the tip of the pencil holding our cut-out up.

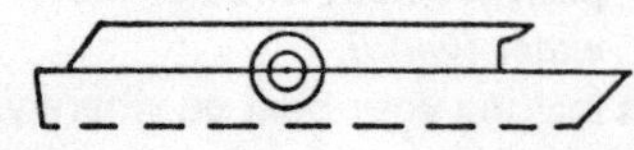

Next we can do the same thing with the bottom half, only here we are talking not of wind but of water.

So mark it with a single ring (to match the single arrowhead for current).

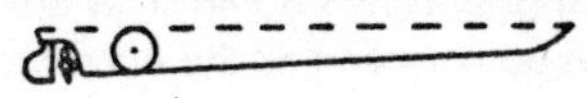

Again we can think of the water as pushing at the middle like the wind did on the top half.

Now put the two halves together again. We can see that the wind and water acting together will tend to *swing* the boat. Water being more resistant than air, the boat will in fact swing round the middle of the lower part. But as the boat swings away from the wind, the helmsman will feel the wind as blowing from a new direction, and the top part as seen from the eye of the wind will have a new shape.

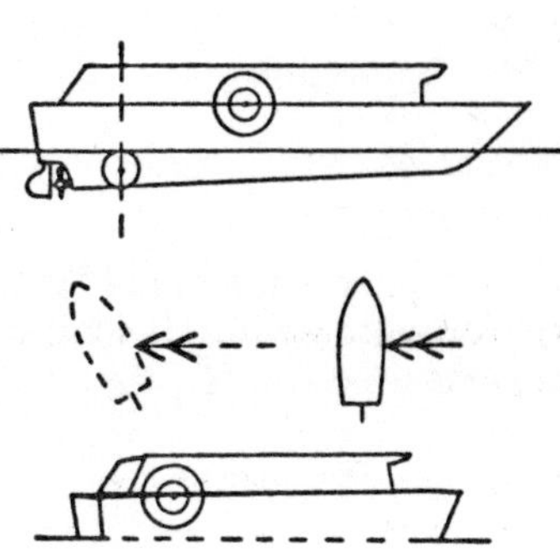

The wind will 'see' more of the stern and less of the bow, so that the effect will be to move the 'middle', where we think of the wind as pushing it, towards the stern.

If you find this difficult to follow, think of the boat as turning right away from the wind. The 'middle' will then be the middle of the stern and the wind will push the boat forwards.

When the middle of the top part has moved back so that it is over the middle of the bottom part, *the boat will stop swinging and drift sideways.*

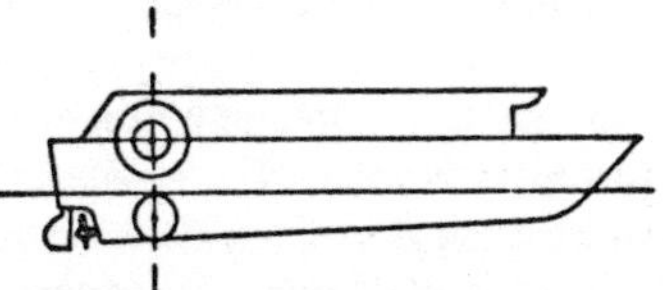

If, however we push the stern sideways, which is in effect what we do when we steer a powerboat, we alter these relationships and the boat tends to pivot about a point much nearer the bows. *The wind and current are working on your boat like this all the time.*

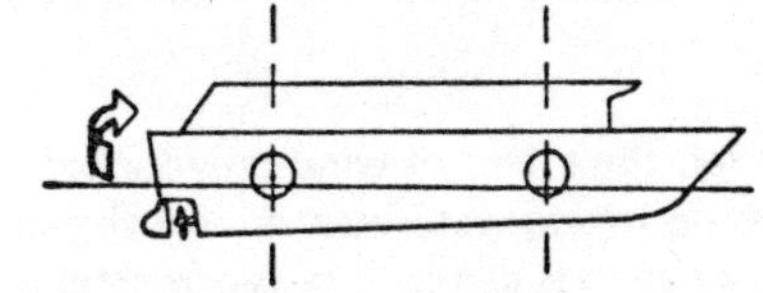

Axis of natural swing *Axis of steering swing*

Suppose now you go slow ahead, at the same speed as the current. If you do not steer this is what will happen.

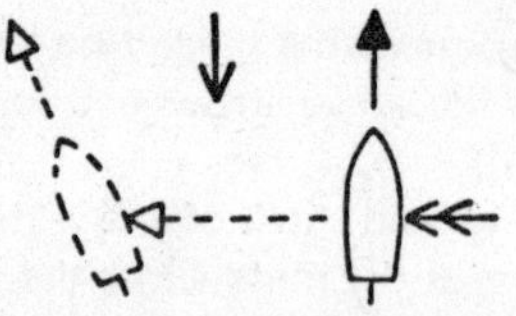

But you are using the engine to make the boat move through the water, so there is water flowing past the rudder and you can steer – you have 'steerage way'.

A boat which is stationary in the water is always out of control because it cannot be steered.

Now turn the wheel to the right, clockwise (to starboard) a bit, to stop the wind swinging the boat.

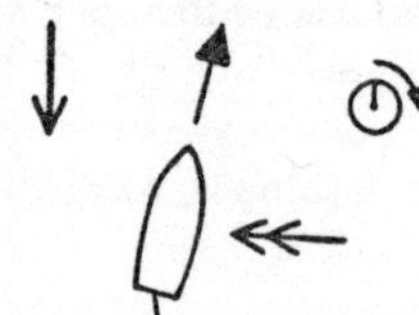

Turn the wheel a bit more to the right to make the boat head slightly into the wind.

You have now learnt *how to make the boat stay in the same place.* Increase speed and you start moving past the land in the direction you want to go. Practise this for yourself, and you will quickly learn how to allow for wind and current. Remember:

Current/tide Imagine you are on an escalator and see a poster of a beautiful woman. The escalator will carry you past the poster at its own speed even if you are dancing about for joy or trying to run backwards down the escalator for a longer look at the poster. This is how the current works on your boat.

Wind The effect of wind on a motorcruiser will be much less than that of current. You can almost forget about head or following winds unless you are mooring or anchoring (see Chapter 6). *Remember to allow for side winds, especially when you are going slowly or manoeuvring.*

You have probably felt the effect of wind on your car on a main road or motorway. Winds on inland waterways funnel through gaps, and the effect of changes in sidewinds can be just as powerful as it is when you overtake a furniture van or pass under a motorway bridge.

Obvious. . .

Less obvious, but just as strong

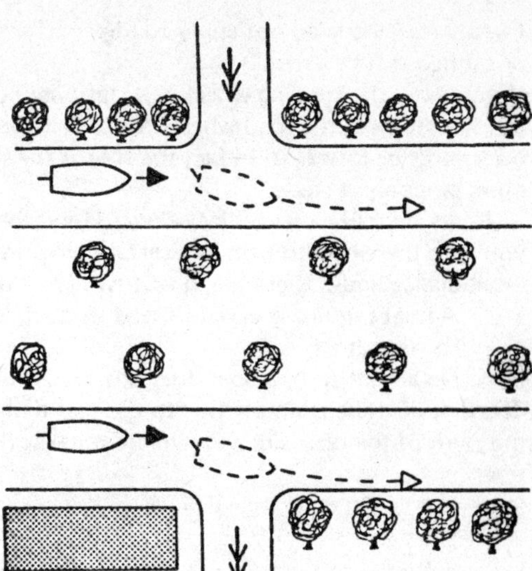

Always leave plenty of room on your downwind ('lee') side.

Changing speed

Just as on a car, to go faster you open the throttle. A motorcruiser will respond more slowly than a family car. Always keep a bit in hand; the last inch or two of throttle lever costs a lot of fuel and the extra power goes into making more wash and very little extra speed.

In a car, or more particularly a lorry, you change into a low forward gear down steep, long hills 'to use the engine as a brake' – to help the brakes out. In a boat you have no brakes or low gears. But because water 'gives' you can brake by changing into reverse gear. Opening the throttle then puts the brakes on harder.

But *don't* change between forward and reverse with the engine revving. With single-lever control (combined gear lever and throttle) pause a moment in neutral. With separate controls, close the throttle, change gear and open the throttle again.

Since your engine is also your only brake, things get difficult if it cuts out or fails to respond. Warm up both petrol and diesel engines before you move off.

Steering

The remarks below apply to low/medium powered boats with a single fixed screw. They do not apply to high performance boats, twin screws or outboard type drives.

If you twist the steering wheel of a stationary car, nothing happens; but the moment the road wheels turn at all the car will steer normally backwards or forwards. In fact the slower the speed the sharper and more precisely it steers.

Boats steer like cars both backwards and forwards as far as the way you turn the wheel to turn in a certain direction goes: but there the resemblance ends. There are in fact two key differences:

1 A boat requires a certain speed through the water ('steerage way') to steer at all.

2 On a tight turn, a boat does not 'track round', but pivots.

The first of these is simply due to the fact that the rudder will not push the stern of the boat sideways unless water is flowing past it.

On a shallow turn the boat will 'track round' more or less like a car; although because the rudder is at the back, a boat going forward steers like a car going backwards and vice versa.

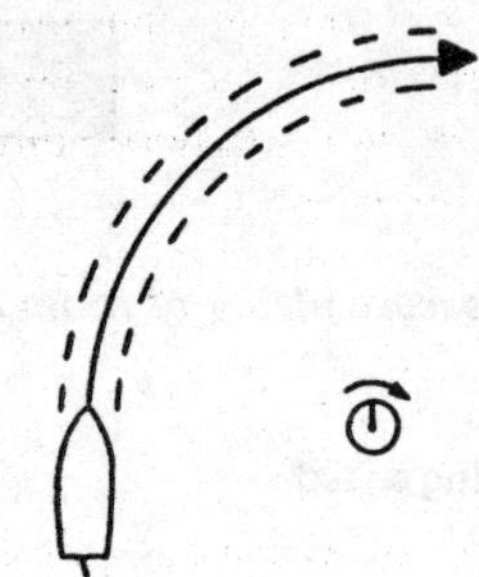

But if the rudder is turned through more than about 45°, the boat will pivot about a point near the bow. As the boat goes one way, its stern sticks out the other.

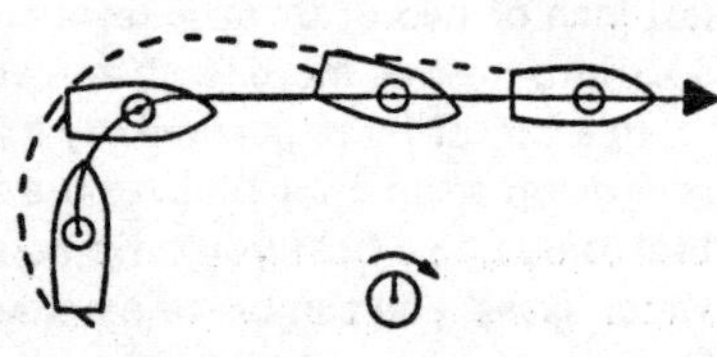

This makes it futile and dangerous to try and turn sharply when you are too near a bank or when you are leaving a mooring. You hope. . .

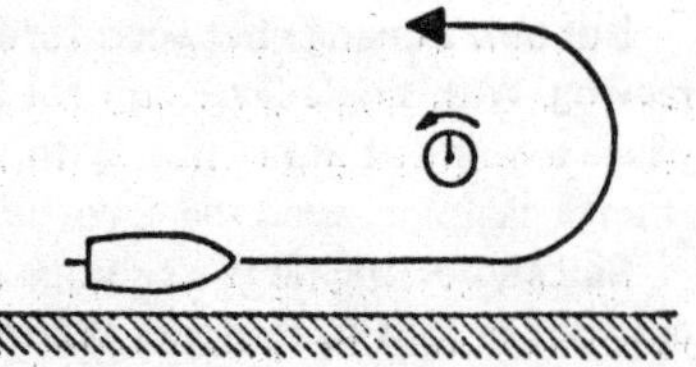

But what happens might be described as the 'Dodgems' syndrome. . .
. . . your stern simply grinds along the bank.

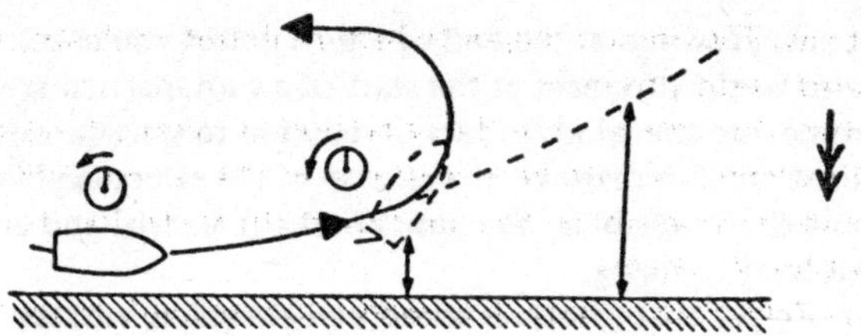

Ease out until there is at least half a boat's length between you and the bank *before* you put the helm over hard. With an onshore wind, allow more. Because water 'gives', once you have got a boat swinging, it will go on swinging.

So straighten up progressively well before you complete the turn and then just 'check' the boat by a slight turn in the opposite direction.

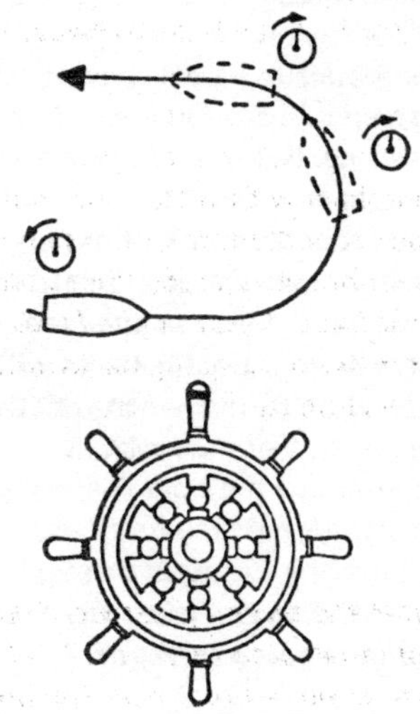

Many boats' wheels have a thick or grooved spoke or similar mark which is upright when the rudder is straight.

The ways engine and boat speed affect turning depend on the design of hull and the positions and shapes of propellor and rudder. You can make most boats turn sharply by giving a 'stab' of throttle as you start turning the wheel and then throttling right back as the boat starts swinging. But there are a few designs, particularly shorter boats, which react differently and have to be turned at very low engine speeds.

To make a still tighter turn, start as above and once the boat is swinging engage reverse gear ('go astern') but not so hard or for so long that the boat actually moves backwards. Most boats can be 'turned on a sixpence' in this way.

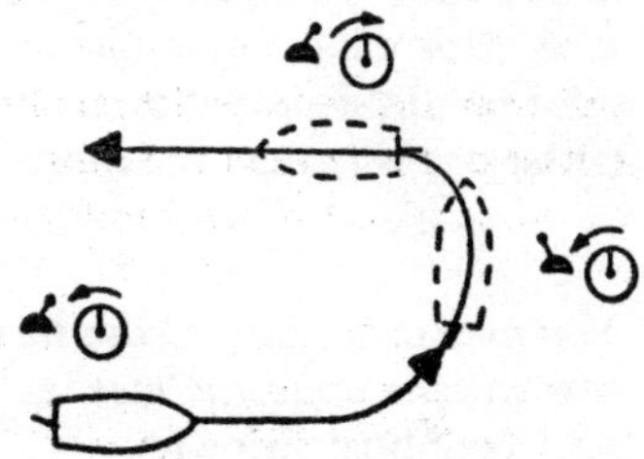

A boat always swings at the end of a turn unless you check it; it may often also be slow to react at the start of a turn, particularly when you are turning into the wind. In fact, it may fail to start swinging and just go straight on. The reason is the reverse of the effect explained at the beginning of this chapter. You must find out by trial and error how to get your boat swinging.

Don't forget that whatever speed you are going, whatever course you are heading or manoeuvre you are making, wind and current will go on working their will on the boat. Make ample allowance for this – give yourself plenty of time and space.

Going astern

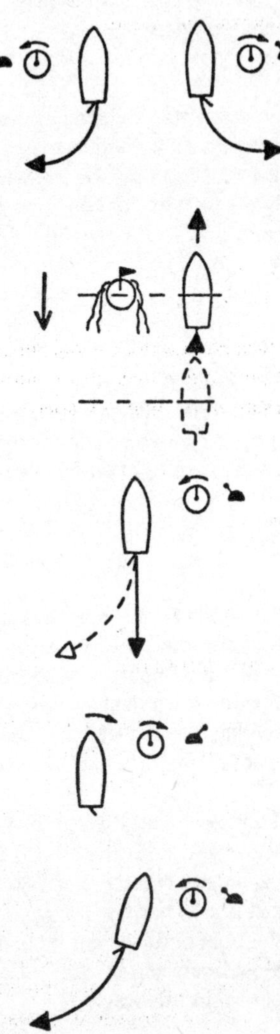

Theoretically a boat moving astern is steered in the same way as a car reversing. But in practice it's seldom quite as easy as that.

You probably think of moving forwards or backwards in relation *to some fixed object or the land.* But the way your boat behaves will depend on its movement relative to the *water*. For example. . .

To your eye the boat is moving *backwards* past the *buoy.* But it is still moving *forwards* through the *water* and so *you must steer it as if you were going forwards.*

If you engage forward gear and accelerate slightly, the boat comes under control ('gathers steerage way') almost at once.

When going astern, it takes a lot longer to get steerage way on, and many boats need very firm handling to start them swinging at all.

Also, depending on the direction of rotation of the propellor, boats turn better one way than the other.

You may often have to use forward gear and the opposite 'lock' to start your boat swinging.

Going astern 'on full lock' and even more, changing from one 'lock' to the other with the throttle wide open puts a heavy strain on the rudder; and the boat may not respond. In the manoeuvre shown here, the action at* is:

Close throttle in good time
Wheel over
Reopen throttle a little

If necessary give a stab ahead to reverse the swing.

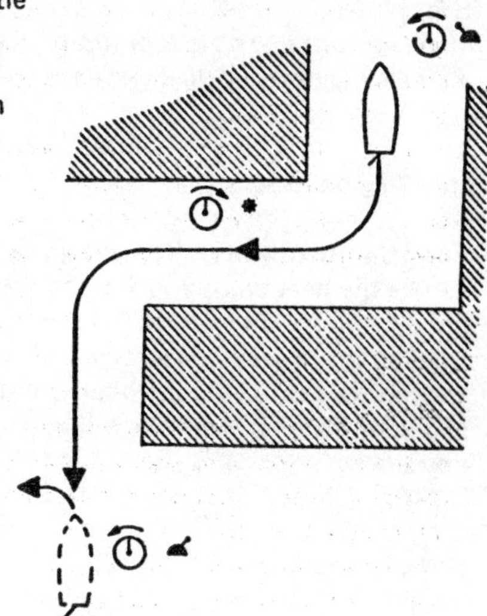

Because the boat is harder to handle and less predictable when going astern make even more allowance for the effects of wind and tide – even more time and space.

Turning round

You can make a three (or more) point turn in a boat just as you can in a car. Having got the boat swinging, you want to keep it swinging the same way, *so between moves 1 and 2 keep 'full lock' on, engage reverse gear and then turn quickly from lock to lock when the boat starts moving backwards.* But between 2 and 3, put the wheel over *before* engaging forward gear.

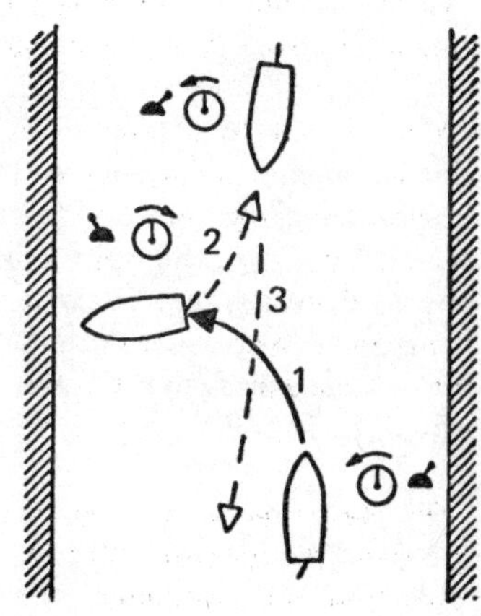

This idea of the boat swinging or pivoting in the water is quite different from the way a car behaves, and is the key to manoeuvring a boat in tight places.

Never turn just upstream (up-tide) of a bridge or other obstruction. You may get carried down onto it.

Handling on ropes

For manoeuvring in really tight spaces it is often safest and quickest to handle the boat on ropes from the shore or other moored boats. This is not an admission of defeat! It is very seamanlike and great fun. But if wind and/or current are strong, make sure you and your crew have enough *weight* to hold the boat against them. It is weight that counts, and your children, however willing, may be much less effective than you think.

Night navigation

Night navigation is generally forbidden for hire craft. Private powerboats used at night must have *navigation lights* (masthead, side – red and green – and stern). A riding light (white all round) should be shown

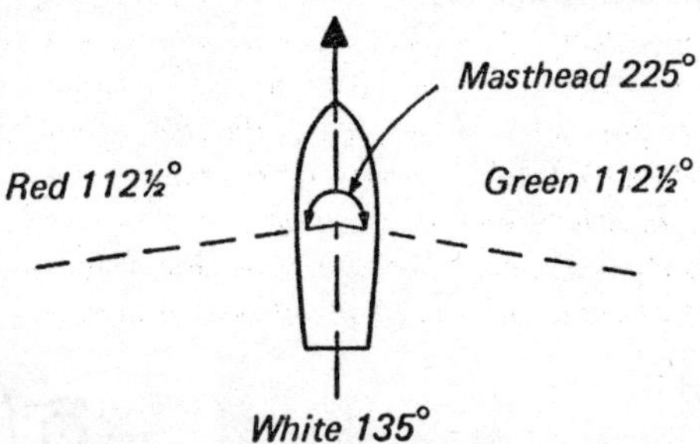

when at anchor. You may need another light or a torch to see detail for manoeuvring, etc., but don't use it as a headlight and don't dazzle others. Your eyes will quickly adapt to the dark and you will find you can see the water quite clearly. Close one eye when you use a torch or flame to keep your eyes adapted.

Go slowly and always leave plenty of margin until you are used to navigating at night. In particular, go dead slow past moored boats.

3 Navigational marks

Channel markers

Channels are marked with posts. The *starboard* side of the channel is defined as *the side to your right as you move away from the sea.* Starboard markers are *black* with white tops. *Port* markers, on the left as you move away from the sea, are *red.*

Channel junction markers are striped – black and white if the main channel is the left fork, *red and white* if the main channel is the right fork. You leave junction markers to either side, depending on which channel you are taking. But make sure you stay inside the channel. *Don't* cut across the wrong side of the junction marker.

So when you are heading *away from the sea,* you leave *black to your right, red to your left.* When you are heading *towards the sea,* leave *black to your left, red to your right.*

Sometimes channels are marked on one side only. *In this case stay as close to the markers are your right of way allows.*

There is usually a good reason for a dogleg in a marked channel. *Don't* cut across it.

Fixed post marker: PORT (red)

Fixed post marker: STARBOARD (black with white tip)

Disc buoy marker: PORT (red)

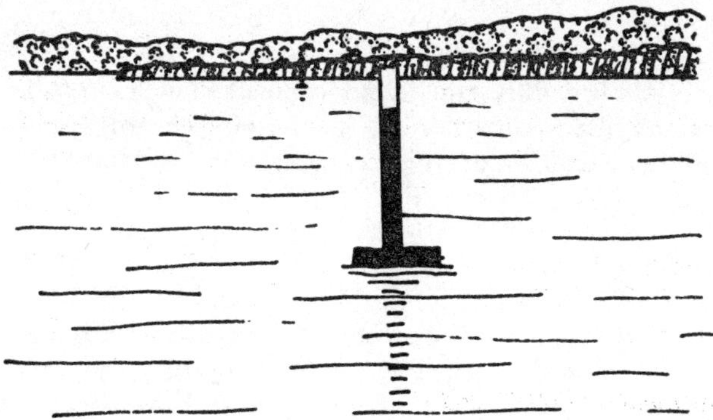

Disc buoy marker: STARBOARD (black with white tip)

Channel intersection marker: red/white or black/white

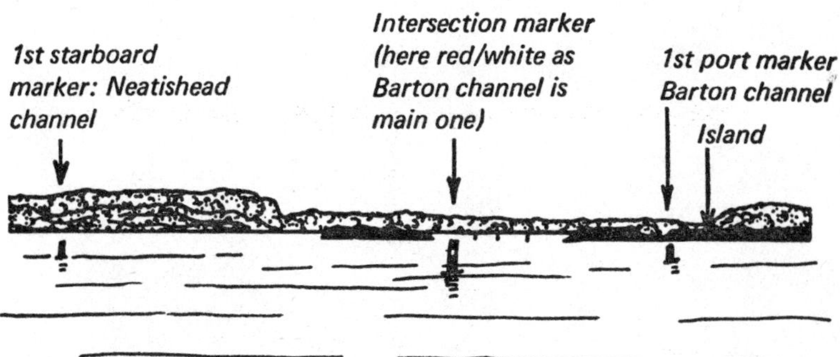

South entrance to Barton Broad

Hazards

On the Norfolk Broads system hazards are marked with *red flags.* There are very often warning or explanatory noticeboards also – *slow down and read these,* but don't go too close onto the hazard.

Racing marks

Racing marks are usually spherical or conical *yellow* or *orange* buoys with small triangular flags on. They have no navigational meaning, but in crowded waters they will indicate to you where sailing boats are likely to be turning.

4 Rule of the road

Navigation on the Norfolk Broads system is not subject to the International Rule of the Road, but to local byelaws. These rules are designed for narrow waterways and are therefore more like driving rules than is the International Rule. Also, although you drive on the right, 'Broads priority' is more like the British Highway Code while the International Rule resembles Continental driving codes.

Since many skippers and helmsmen may either be under the impression that the International Rule applies or will react instinctively in accordance with the International Rule in emergency, the existence of these special rules calls for special care from everyone in charge of a boat. On the other hand, inexperienced skippers who can drive a car will find them easy to follow.

General principle

Always act in such a way as to avoid a collision, i.e. with another boat or with a fixed object. This is the boating equivalent of 'defensive driving'.

Basic rules

Keep in the RIGHT HAND half of the waterway (like driving on the Continent), i.e. boats pass left side (port) to left side.

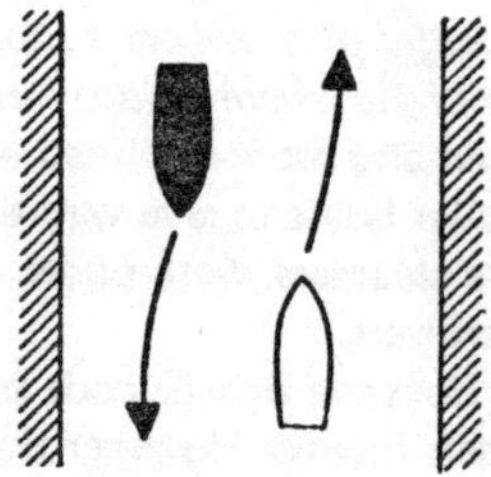

Boats moving ACROSS a waterway or marked channel GIVE WAY to boats moving ALONG it. On open waters without a marked channel, the right-of-way direction is considered to be the general direction between one entrance and another, or, in the case of a dead end, a projection of the line of the entrance channel.

Powerboats moving AGAINST THE TIDE must be prepared to give way to boats moving WITH THE TIDE at:

A point or sharp bend

A bridge or other channel too narrow for two boats to pass.

The boat moving against the tide must be prepared to stop or go astern is necessary.

Any boat OVERTAKING any other boat must keep OUT OF THE WAY of the boat being overtaken. Any boat approaching another one from within the hatched sector is considered to be an overtaking boat (this is in effect the same as the International Rule provision on giving way to all craft ahead).

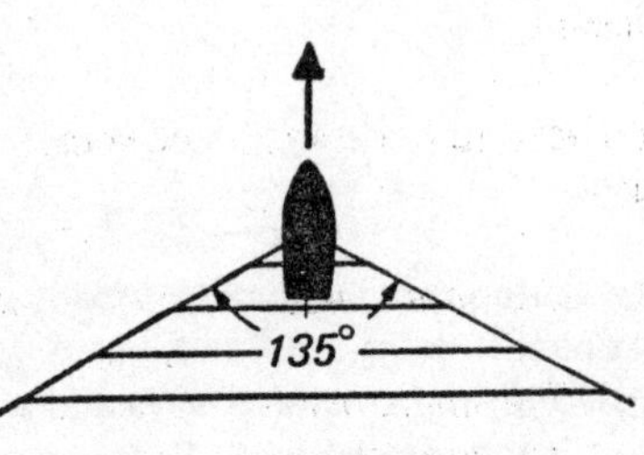

The give way craft should alter course and speed in good time and *avoid crossing the bows of the right-of-way vessel.* The right-of-way craft should hold its course and speed until all risk of collision is past (see also under 'Overtaking' below).

Priorities

Boats under sail have priority over boats under power, except when:

1 A boat is using engine as well as sail, when it is considered to be under power (but remember it may have its engine running in neutral).

2 A boat under sail is overtaking a boat under power.

'Narrow channel rights' as generally understood and defined are not included in the Broads code, although rather similar provisions do apply to powered vessels over 100 feet long, i.e. coasters navigating the Yare. *In particular pleasure craft should give way to large vessels for which Carrow or Reedham Bridge has been opened.* However, particularly in shallower and more confined waters, it is both sensible and courteous for smaller boats to give way to larger ones such as tugs, barges, pleasure steamers, waterbuses, and the larger seagoing yachts and motorcruisers.

Nor does the Broads code provide any specific overriding priority for vessels towing. However the code includes a warning to give them a wide berth, and common sense and courtesy suggest that every allowance should be made for their limited powers of manoeuvre.

Rowing dinghies do not have any specific rights, but powerboats should treat them as the pedestrians of the water, keeping well clear and slowing down so that the wash does not swamp them.

Nor do swimmers and water skiers who have come off have any legal rights, but there is an overriding duty on all craft to keep a lookout for them and to keep clear unless they require help. Don't hesitate to hail a dinghy or a swimmer which you may think may not have seen you ('Ahead dinghy', 'Ahead swimmer', etc.).

Signals

You need to understand and sometimes to use the following sound signals:

One short blast	I am altering course to my RIGHT (starboard)
Two short blasts	I am altering course to my LEFT (port).
Three short blasts	My engines are going astern
Four short blasts	I am unable to manoeuvre

Other signals, seldom used but worth knowing in case a large craft gives them, are:

Four short followed by one short	I am making a U-turn to the RIGHT (starboard)
Four short followed by two short	I am making a U-turn to the LEFT (port).

Use *one long blast* to give warning of your presence.

However, in waters crowded with a lot of pleasure craft it is often difficult to tell which boat has made a sound signal and therefore more sensible to give a hand signal and/or a hail (when hailing another boat, start with 'Ahoy'). *Don't* be shy about hailing.

Use whatever form of hand signal you think will be clearest. The Highway Code signals are widely understood. *A powerboat should always signal its own intention,* like a car, but *yachts* can and often do help powerboats past them by signalling which side they want the powerboat to go. *No signal gives you a right of way you would not otherwise have.*

Manoeuvres

To a far greater extent than on the road your right of way depends on your maintaining course and speed or turning only to conform to a channel — staying in the traffic stream, so to speak. *Anything you do other than this is a 'manoeuvre', and any craft making a manoeuvre must keep clear of ALL other craft,* unless it is forced to take avoiding action through no fault of its own, in which case it must make a sound signal or hail.

There are some important special cases of manoeuvres:

Leaving moorings/weighing anchor

This is a manoeuvre, and you must *wait until you can move off without interfering with any craft already under way* (like a parked car moving off).

Overtaking

Both under the basic rules and because overtaking is a manoeuvre, *an overtaking boat has an absolute responsibility to keep clear both of the boat being overtaken and of any oncoming traffic* until it is completely clear of the overtaking boat and the latter can manoeuvre freely. You must also make sure that your wash will not inconvenience any other boat, in particular that it will not sweep an overtaken yacht or dinghy onto the bank. *You are fully liable for any damage or injury whatever that results directly or indirectly from your overtaking manoeuvre.*

Speed differences on the water are much smaller than on the road. Make sure you have plenty of time and space to overtake. You can overtake on either side, but if you are cutting through on the inside, i.e. leaving the overtaken boat on your left, make sure you will not create a dangerous situation or inconvenience moored boats, fishermen, etc.

Turning at a junction

If you are on a major waterway and entering a smaller one to your *right* (starboard) you should normally have a clear passage (but see Chapter 2).

If the waterway you are entering is on your *left* (port), you should slow down, pull across to the centre of the waterway and wait until your path is clear of oncoming traffic, exactly as you would when turning right in a car. (This is an important difference from the usual interpretation of the International Rule).

Entering a large waterway from a minor one

A craft entering a major waterway from a minor one *must give way* to craft on the major one. Some of these junctions, particularly in built-up areas, are completely blind and boats on the major waterway should also keep a good lookout.

U-turns

Hold speed and course until the waterway is clear of oncoming traffic, then signal your intention and make your turn. *Make sure you have enough clearance from the near (starboard) bank* (Chapter 2).

Don't make a U-turn across the bows of an overtaking boat which has already started its manoeuvre.

Accidents

If you are involved in an accident you should stop, give every possible assistance to the other craft and exchange names and addresses, etc., as you would in a motor accident. *Remember the saving of life takes precedence over the salving of property.*

5 Right-of-way problems

The density of traffic on the Broads, the large number of yachts and the narrowness of a few of the waterways can call for a measure of give and take regarding the right of way if accidents, or at least crises, are to be avoided.

General

Remember your overriding responsibility for acting so as to avoid collisions. *Don't* try to carve your way through dense traffic, especially if there are a lot of dinghies about. *Watch out* for other boats starting a manoeuvre. They may not have seen you, or they may think they have enough room. Life will be much easier for everyone if you stand well off and let them complete their manoeuvre.

It is customary to take your *fenders* in when under way. But there is a dispensation for boats operating in congested waters, and many Broads skippers prefer to leave their fenders in position. If you do this, make sure they are secure and not trailing in the water.

Narrow waterways

On very narrow waterways with passing bays, e.g. Waxham Cut, *don't* go beyond a bay until you can see that your way to the next one is clear. (Just as you would on single-track roads in Devon or the Highlands.)

Before taking a long boat up a narrow waterway, e.g. Lime Kiln Dyke off Barton Broad, check on the map or index that there is room for you to turn at the top. *Don't* try to turn unless you are sure the dyke is wide enough; if you get stuck across a dyke with wooded banks, getting clear is tedious, can sometimes be really difficult and is very likely to damage the boat.

If two powerboats meet where there is not room to pass normally, it is sensible for the larger one to pull into the bank, and let the smaller one manoeuvre.

Sailing races

There is a lot of racing on the broads themselves, but some on the rivers too. A racing fleet on a river is not unlike (fellow yachtsmen please forgive!) a herd of cows on a road. If you are *meeting* it, the best thing to do is to pull over to the bank and go dead slow until clear. If you *come up behind it,* you may be able to cut through, but it is usually less nerve-racking and safer to settle down and follow until the fleet turns or thins out. Turns for racing dinghies are marked by a small buoy with a flag.

Yachts may have to give way to others, and in particular a racing fleet may produce sudden forced manoeuvres in cruising yachts, to which you may in turn have to respond.

Sailing boats

Yachts are often forced by conditions of wind and tide to sail a particular course, maybe a zigzag one, and you should always give them as much space and time as you can.

Yacht skippers or helmsmen will very often indicate to you which side they would like you to pass. You will help yourself and them by complying briskly unless you can see some reason for not doing so, e.g. oncoming traffic. If you delay, look for a new signal – circumstances may have altered. Oddly enough, yachts are much more under control when there is a good breeze and they are moving fairly fast. When there is little wind, they have great difficulty both in steering and in avoiding being swept down on the current.

Yachts wanting to sail into the wind have to 'tack' or zigzag from one side to the other. This is very difficult for large yachts in narrow rivers, especially if the current is against them. And it is very irritating for you!

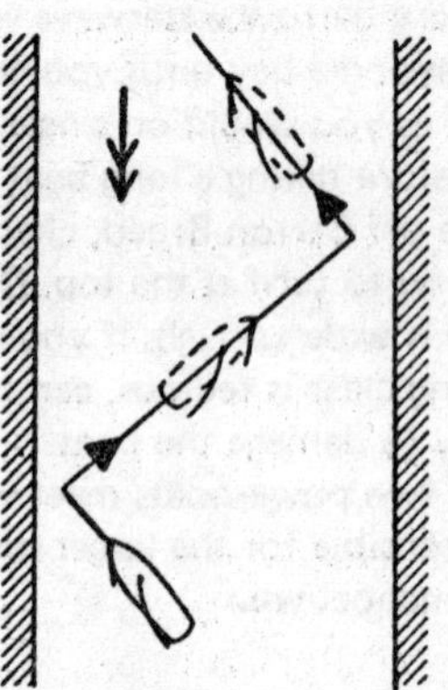

When approaching any yacht, slow down to give yourself time and space to get your boat completely under control. Once you have decided to go, manoeuvre firmly and resume cruising speed.

If you come up behind a yacht that is tacking, *steer as if to follow it then pass behind it as it moves away from the bank. Don't* cut in front of it; it may be making a short tack straight across the river.

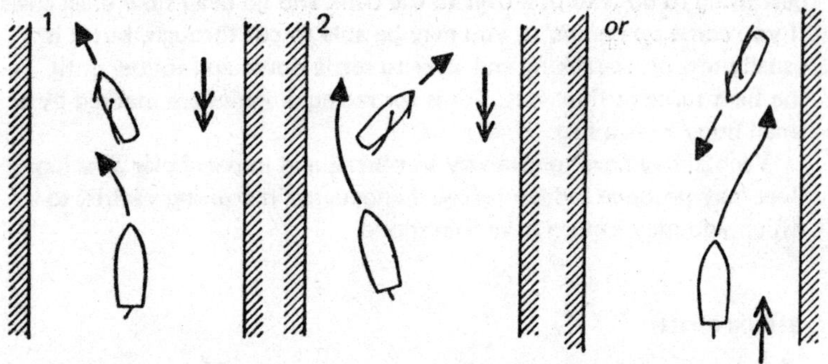

If you meet a yacht that is tacking, *slow right down and steer towards the bank.* Wait until the yacht tacks and then pass behind it. Never try to cut straight across a yacht's bows — the 'sharp end' of a yacht, par-

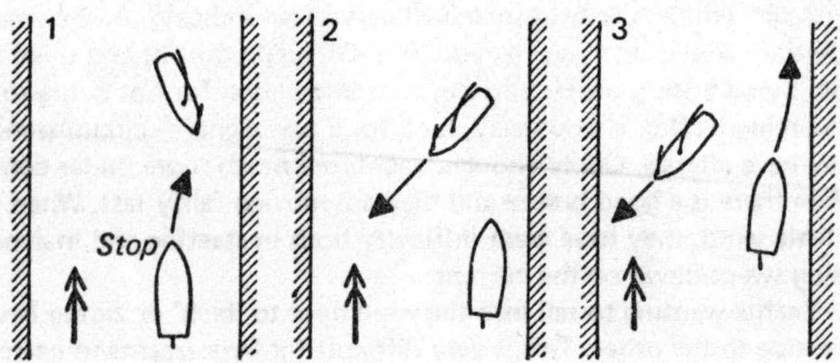

ticularly a Broads yacht, is likely to be just that!

But these are only general tips; you must work out each situation on its merits, but remember:

Slow down – to improve control
– to gain time and space
Manoeuvre firmly – once you have decided what to do
Don't forget – other powerboats might have right of way over you.

When the mixture of boats and lack of space makes it difficult to apply the normal Rule of the Road:

POWERBOATS FOLLOWING YACHTS SHOULD GIVE WAY TO POWERBOATS MEETING THE YACHTS.
THE POWERBOAT WHICH CAN CLEAR THE YACHT WITHOUT CROSSING FROM ITS OWN SIDE OF THE CHANNEL SHOULD GO FIRST.

These suggestions are in accordance with the Rule of the Road, but it may take too long to work them out from the basic rules.

These encounters get very complicated and even hilarious. But they are perfectly safe as long as everyone is patient and no-one tries to carve the party up.

6 Mooring and anchoring

Mooring and anchoring can be difficult and tedious, and even disastrous if you do not know how to *use wind and current to help you;* if you do, they are quick and easy.

The only brake you have on your boat is reverse gear. The first secret of mooring and anchoring is to *use wind and current as extra brakes,* i.e. you head into them, or into whichever of them is the stronger.

The second secret of mooring is to get *BOTH ENDS of the boat under control with ropes* the moment you lose steerage way, or just before.

Wind and current

There are four basic situations. . .

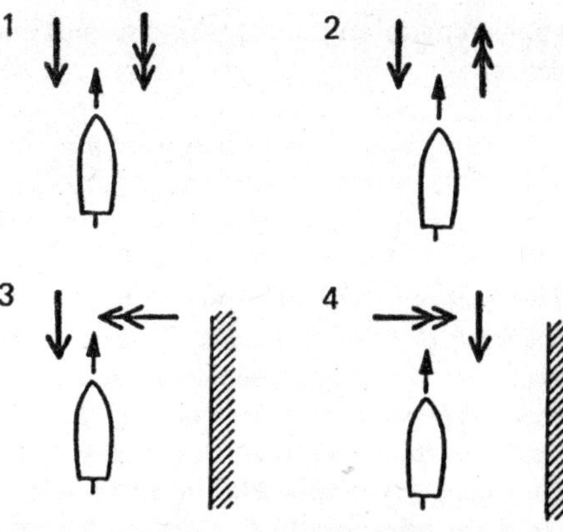

We can think of current as running down the page because, with one exception, *you always moor head to current.* So, if you are moving with the current, turn first. The exception is in Situation 2 when the wind is strong and the current weak.

Remember the relative effects of wind and current on a powerboat.

To find out where the wind is, look at a flag on shore or on a moored boat – not at your own if you are moving. To find out which way the current is, look for a floating object and note which way it is moving. Alternatively note the pattern of ripples from a fixed object in the water.

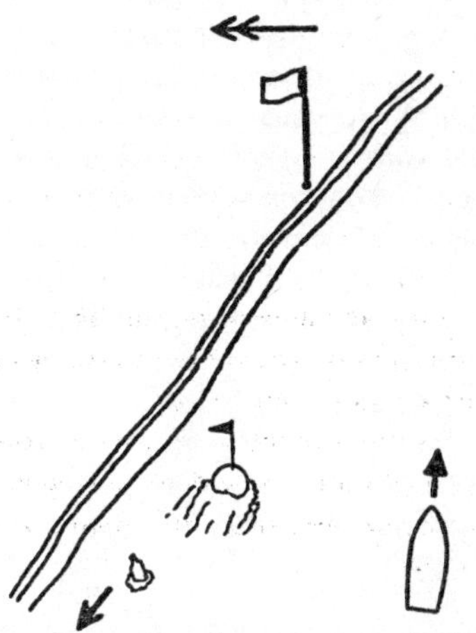

Preparation

You can't just cut into a mooring the way you do a parking meter space. Unless *everything is ready and everyone knows what to do before you go in,* you will either miss the mooring, or hit the bank or another boat – or all three.

Mooring is simplest with a *team of three* – helmsman, bowman, sternman – but it can be done quite safely and easily with two people or single-handed *if you get the ropes in the right place before you go in.* If you are on your own, stop the boat on a quiet piece of water and do your preparation there, making sure of course that you don't drift into danger.

First put out the fenders and adjust them for position or height if necessary. (You may have to adjust them again once you are moored up.) This minimises the risk of damage if you hit something and stops the bow and stern ropes getting under the fender lines and flicking the fenders up at the critical moment. Then get the bow and stern ropes where you want them, making sure they are 'clear', i.e. above/outside anything that could foul them. *Never let ropes trail in the water* — they will foul your propellor. *Note the single-handed drill.* Many accidents occur through the helmsman rushing about the boat at the last moment to pick up ropes!

1 Three men, coming alongside

2 Two or three men, bow first

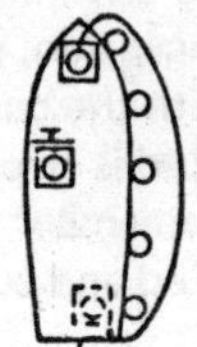

3 Single-handed

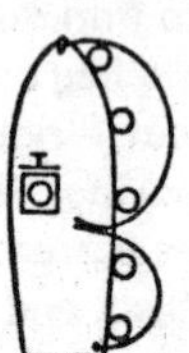

Mooring — still water, no wind

To get the basic drill, suppose you are on a lake on a calm day. You need to know the 'carry' of your boat, how quickly it loses speed and how far it will go after you put the gear in neutral. *This you can only learn by trial and error, but with a powerboat you can give a touch ahead or astern to adjust the carry.*

The art of coming alongside a bank is 'cutting the boat in'. For any boat there is a particular combination of approach speed and angle, timing of manoeuvre and rudder and throttle setting that can only be found by trial and error. *But if you follow this drill and come in SLOWER then you think you should,* you will arrive alongside, if not at first elegantly.

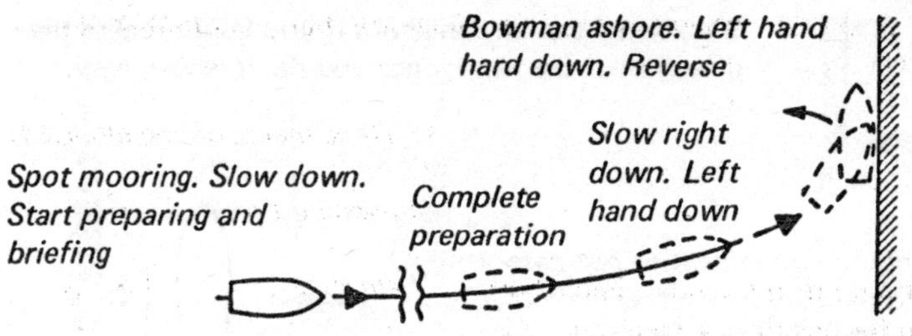

In calm air and still water the boat would theoretically just sit alongside, *but in practice you must secure BOTH ends.* If for any reason you cannot come fully alongside, get the bows secured and pass the stern rope to the man ashore as quickly as possible.

Mooring – wind and current, unobstructed bank

In Situation 1, you need as a rule only give a stab astern to cut your stern in. Wind and current will bring you to rest and hold you in.

In Situation 2, when you have a following wind (or occasionally a following current) *approach even more slowly than normal,* (but keep steerage way on), start going astern before you 'cut' your stern in, and *keep going slow astern,* having straightened the helm, to hold the boat stationary relative to the land. *You must get the stern under control on a rope straightaway or it will swing out* – and it may be very difficult to pull it in again once wind or current starts bearing on your side.

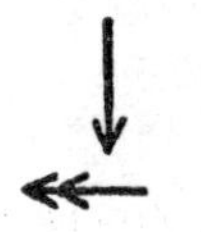

Situation 3 is the safest mooring to go into and the easiest to get off, but it needs *a certain amount of firmness coming in or you will be blown off before you can get a rope ashore.* So make sure you are well fended on the shoulder(*). This does NOT mean you should charge in! The idea to have in your head is *to HOLD the boat against the bank with the engine* for long enough to get your bowman ashore *before* you cut the stern in. If you are single-handed in this situation hold in, cut in, get ashore.

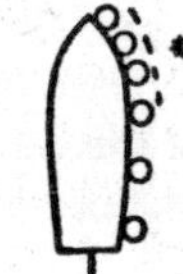

Situation 4 can be dangerous if you fail to realise the direction of the wind; once you do, it is very easy.

Simply bring the boat to rest parallel to the bank and a few feet off it. Allow the wind to take you in. Go slow ahead if needs be to stop the current pushing you back to swinging your bow out.

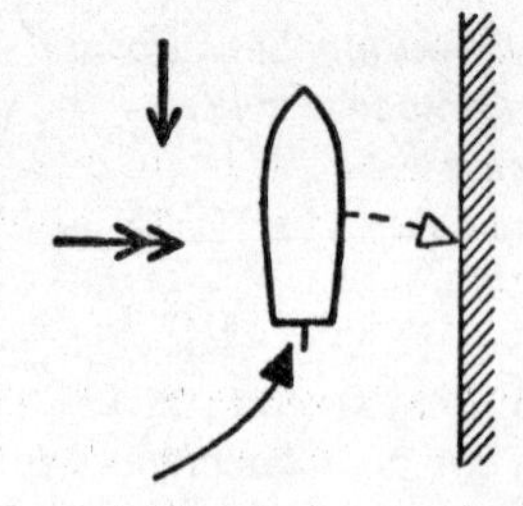

Mooring in a gap

It is accepted custom that you may put a man onto the deck of a boat already moored to get a rope ashore. If there is anyone on board, ask permission – you will usually get help. It is also acceptable to tie up, at least temporarily, alongside another boat, provided the waterway is wide enough for you not to obstruct other traffic by doing so.

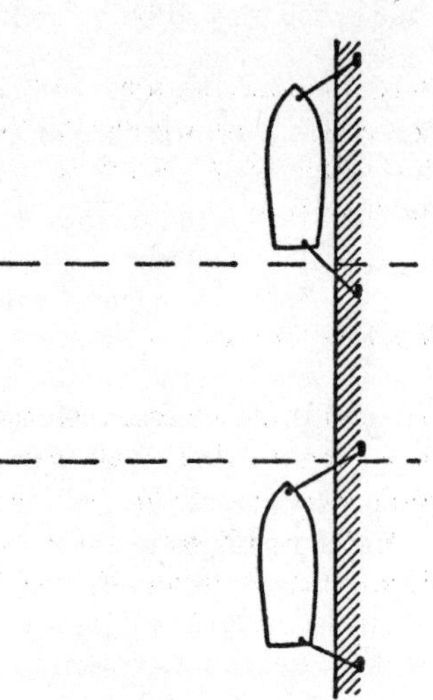

So in cutting into a gap you have to decide whether to go in direct or to get a rope onto another boat and handle your boat in on ropes. With an onshore wind (Situation 4) it is usually easy to get into even a very short gap, as the technique is just a slight stretch of the normal procedure.

With a following wind or current (Situation 2) NEVER attempt to go straight into a gap. Get a man with your ropes onto another boat. The same applies if the wind is anywhere 'abaft the beam'.

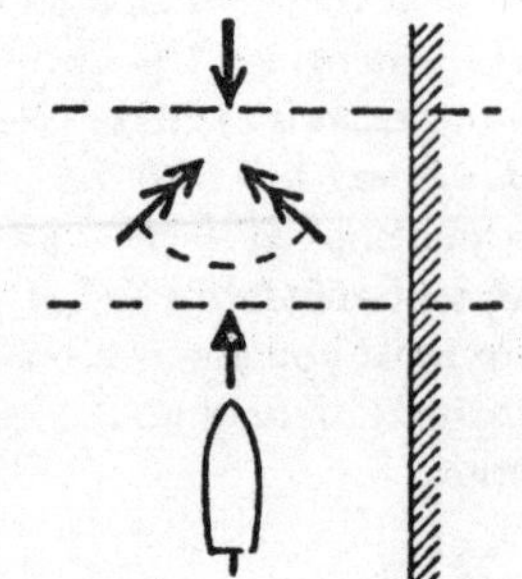

In Situations 1 and 3 or with the wind anywhere 'forward of the beam', you can get into a short gap by *going in bow first* and bringing the stern in on the stern rope:

Make sure your bow and shoulder are well fended.

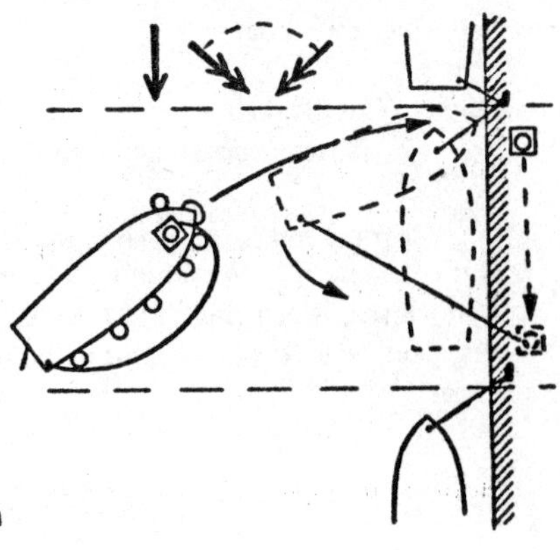

Lay the sternrope to the bow, so that the bowman can take both ashore.

Go in *very slowly bow first,* checking the boat with the engine, to the *upwind/up-current end of the gap.*

Once the bow is secured (not too tightly) the stern will swing in with the current or can be pulled in with the stern rope.

Mooring stern on

In certain authorised places such as basins, dead-ends, etc. (but NEVER on a river or dyke), boats may be moored stern on. If there is plenty of room when you arrive, go in alongside and turn the boat on ropes.

Wherever the wind is, it takes a lot of skill to reverse a motorcruiser down a gap of little more than its own width.

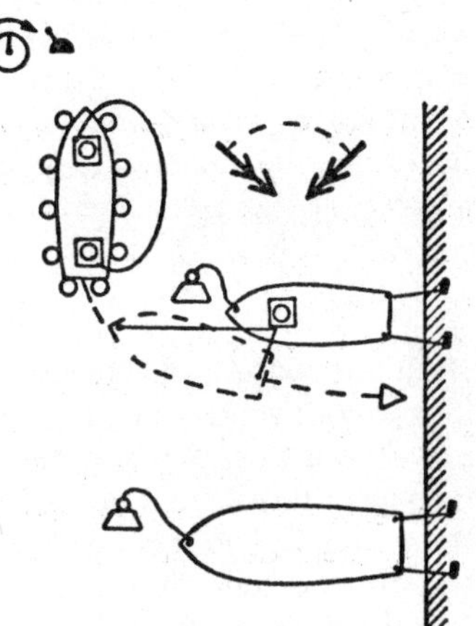

Put fenders along both sides and on the stern. Lay the bow rope to the stern. *Manoeuvre to get a man with both bow and stern ropes onto the foredeck of the boat upwind of the gap.* He can then bring you round and in. Go dead slow astern to help him, and fend/guide the other (downwind) side.

Moor with two stern ropes and an anchor or mudweight at the bow. Drop this *before the last part of your move in,* so that it is well out and upwind of your bow.

Securing your boat

Ropes. The ideal is:

2 mooring ropes each one and a half times the length of the boat;

2 mooring ropes each three times the length of the boat.

But if a rope is long enough you can often make it serve two purposes at once, e.g. stern rope and breast rope (see below), by securing it on the cleat near its middle and using both ends as if they were separate ropes.

Tying a boat up so that it will ride securely and comfortably whatever the direction of wind and current is something of an art – and in tidal waters you also have to allow for the rise and fall of the tide.

In still waters and calm weather, *bow and stern ropes (1 and 2),* led well off to front and rear and left slightly slack, may well suffice. You might want to add one or two *breast ropes (3 and 4)* to hold the boat well in for children to get on and off.

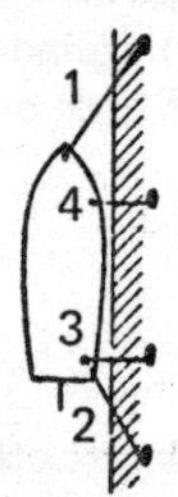

If current and/or wind are strong, if large craft which produce a lot of undertow are passing, or if the tide is going to turn so that you are stern on to it, you may need one or two diagonal ropes known as *'springs'* (5 and/or 6). These stop the end of the boat to which they are attached being swung out.

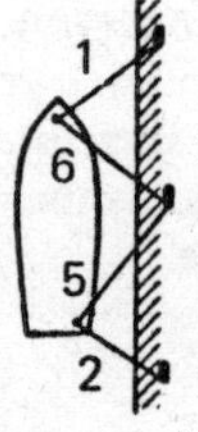

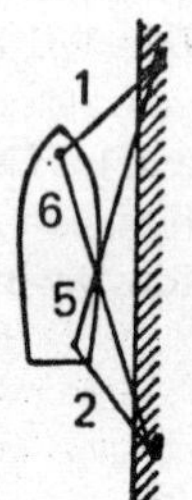

If you moor alongside another boat, you *must have one rope secured ashore* – better two. As a matter of courtesy, always put this/these ropes on the posts *under* any ropes already there, so that other boats can leave without having to undo your ropes.

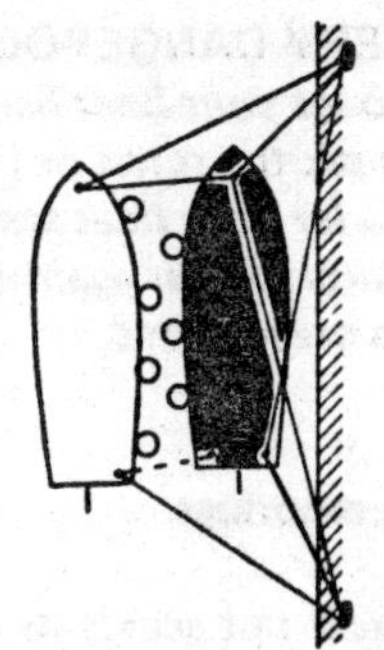

Unless the boat inside you is a yacht, it can usually get out by passing under your ropes. You then adjust these to take its place.

On a crowded *tidal mooring* – except for a pontoon which rises and falls with the tide – it is almost essential to leave someone on board to adjust the ropes as the water rises and falls. Boats left unmanned on a tidal mooring require more space – say two boat-lengths each – so that they can move with the tide without risk of colliding. For simplicity, springs are not shown in the drawing, but they would be necessary in a case like this:

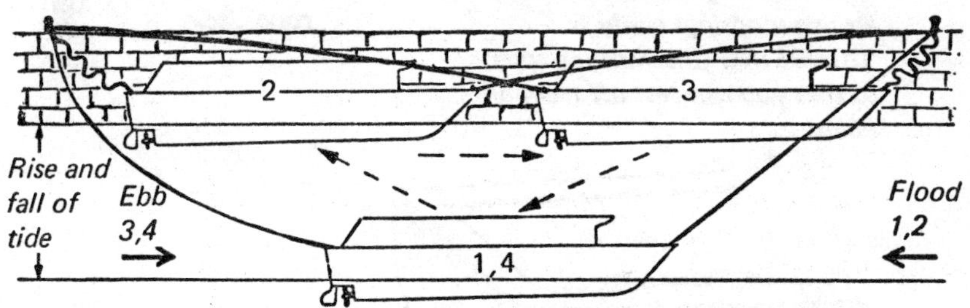

At the same time as adjusting the ropes, you may have to adjust the position of the rudder and lash the wheel or tiller. Remember that the water flowing past the boat has exactly the same effect as the boat moving through the water. So you have "steerage way" when the current is strong, and can use the rudder to keep the boat parallel to the bank.

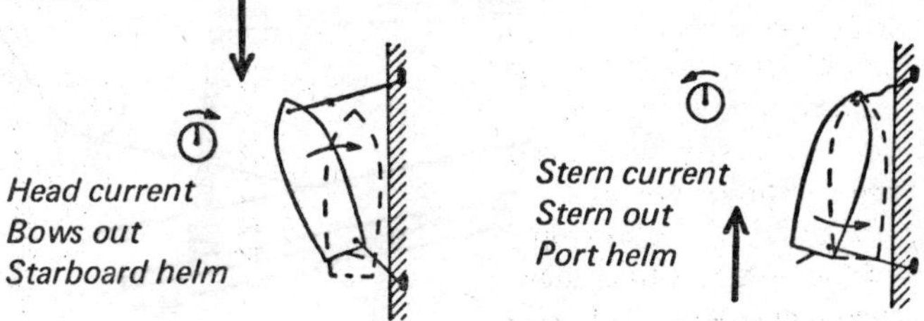

IT IS VERY DANGEROUS:

1 *To let your boat hang on its ropes when the tide falls.* This may break the ropes or fittings and/or capsize the boat.

2 *To let your boat swing out to an angle where a strong current starts to bear against its side.* Adjust the ropes and use the rudder to prevent this.

Leaving moorings

Incidents if not accidents often happen as boats are leaving moorings. This is probably because, unless you follow the right drill, there is a time when your boat is no longer secured to the bank and is not yet under control. *Make sure your crew or helpers on the bank do not cast you off before you are ready.*

Start the engine and *let it warm up.*

Get everyone on board and ready; *those helping you must wear buoyancy aids.*

Clear away and stow any breast ropes or springs. *Look to see which is the working rope. The clue to leaving moorings easily is 'DOUBLING' the working rope, so that you can cast off from on board.*

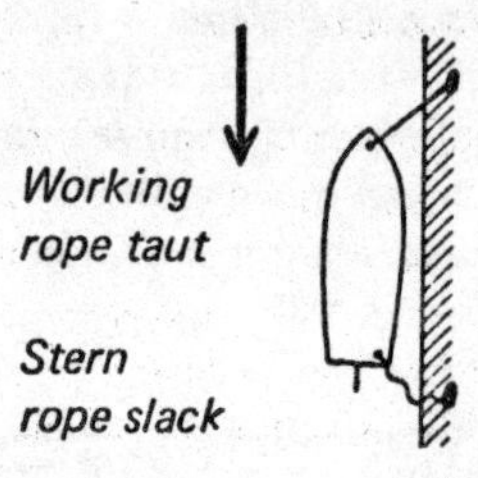

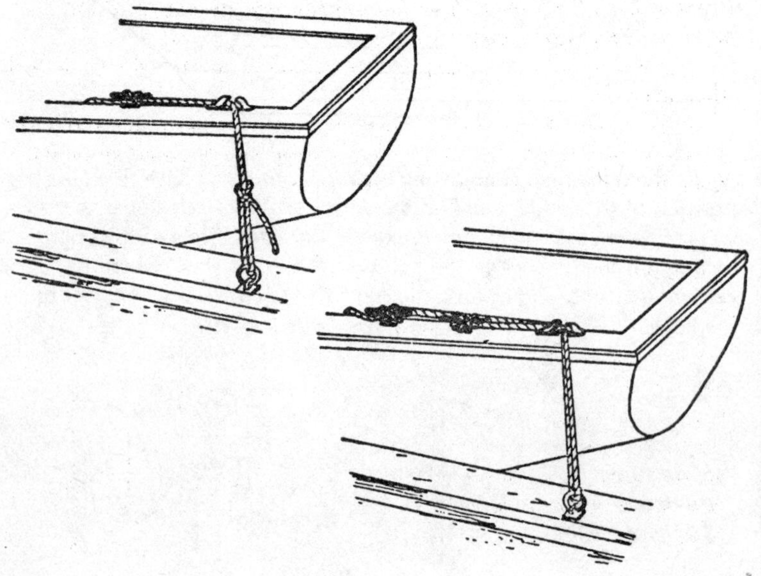

Clear away and coil down or stow the non-working rope. *If there is any risk of your being swung by the wind, get a hold with the boathook. If the non-working rope is the stern rope, DOUBLE-CHECK that it is coiled down or stowed and cannot foul your propellor.*

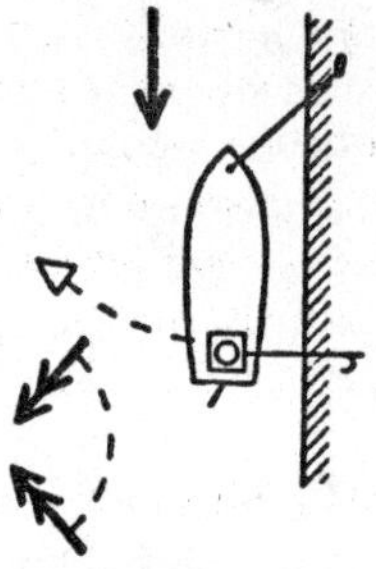

You are now ready to cast off. MAKE SURE THERE IS NOTHING COMING. Give yourself ample time and space.

Situations 1 thru 3

No problem, even if there is a boat moored just ahead of you. You already have steerage way from the current flowing past you. Let yourself go gently down on the current if necessary and if all clear astern.

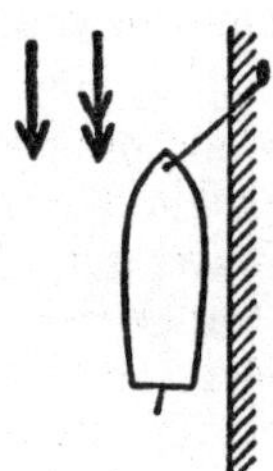

Slow ahead, left hand down — progressively, see page 35. Cast off as soon as the bow rope begins to slacken.

Don't turn out too sharply and swing your stern into the bank or the boat ahead!

It may sometimes be safer and easier to go out stern first, but make sure you have plenty of room to get steerage way and then bring the boat under control and turn the bow out.

Situation 2

The wind will tend to force your stern out and stop you turning away from the bank. If the current is strong and there is no obstruction ahead, you will be able to get good steerage way quickly. *But ease well out before turning sharply.*

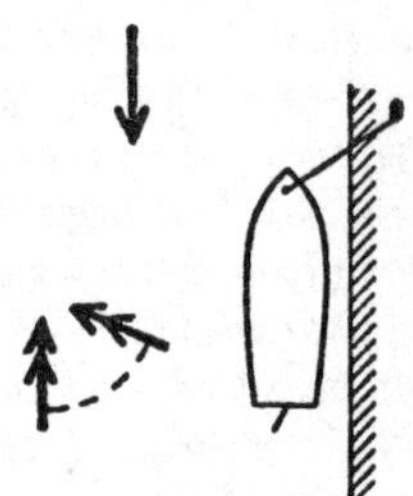

If there is any obstruction ahead, get the bowman to push the bow out with his feet or the boathook as he casts off. If the wind is well on the beam (offshore) rather than following, you can simply hold the boat against the current (slow ahead) while you drift out sideways.

Situation 4

Getting off a 'lee shore' needs a bit of skill and care, especially if there are obstructions ahead or astern of you.

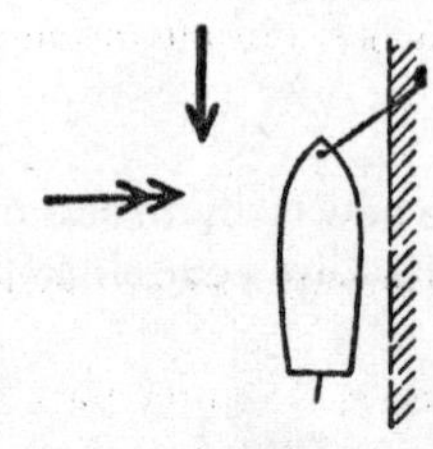

If you have plenty of room astern, it is probably safest, if rather inelegant, to go out stern first. The steering reaction will not then hold the boat against the bank, but of course the wind may prevent it from starting to swing.

If the bank ahead is clear, *push the bows out with the boathook,* and *gradually* power out, fending as necessary. Put on more throttle and rudder as clearance(*) increases.

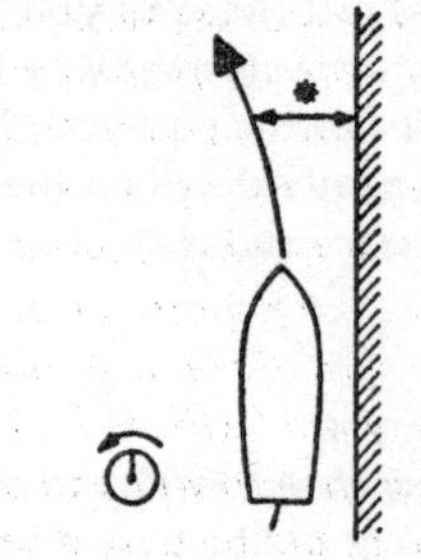

Getting out of a gap can be distinctly awkward. Get your stern well fended. This is one of the few cases where you may need to *put a man ashore.* Get him to *take the stern rope forward as a spring. Cast off the bow and let the current take the bow out, first from the bank and then (gently!) from the stern of the boat ahead of you. At the same time get the man on the bank to pull the stern up to himself; and go slow ahead, left hand hard down.*

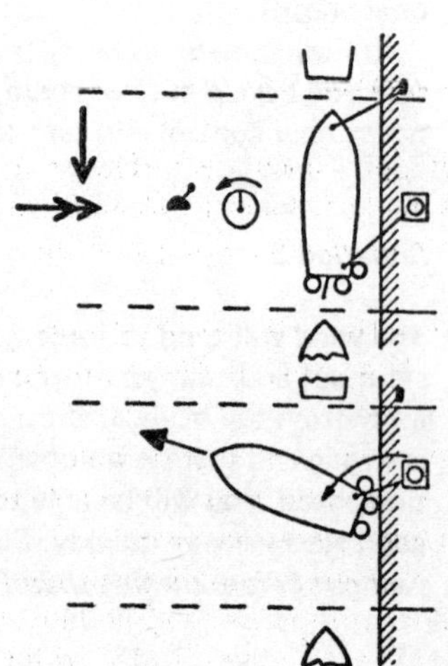

The current will start swinging your bow out and you will pivot about your stern. *The man ashore must get aboard quickly with the rope, keeping it taut,* or you will be swung right round onto the boat astern of you. *The moment he is aboard, go RIGHT hand down, full ahead* until you have got control.

If there is a mooring post roughly opposite the bow and you have a long enough rope, it is of course much easier to double the stern rope on to that as a spring and control it from on board, pulling it in and clear at the appropriate moment.

Leaving moorings stern to current

In tidal waters, you may have come in head to current but want to go out when the current is on your stern. This can cause difficulties, and it is often wise to *turn the boat on ropes when the tide is slack.* Otherwise, the stern rope will now be the working rope.

If there is no obstruction astern, i.e. up-current, you can follow the drills given above, *treating the stern as if it were the bow – but leave yourself plenty of room!* Once you have gained room to manoeuvre, you can turn head to current and move off normally.

If there is an obstruction, you can use the drill given for getting out of a gap on a lee shore (Situation 4 above), *treating the bow as if it were the stern. But make sure the man you put ashore is agile enough to get on board QUICKLY over the bow. Once the tide starts working on your stern, you will swing very quickly.* Likewise a particularly neat way is to spring the bow (the reverse of the drill given above).

Anchoring

Dropping anchor is forbidden in rivers and other narrow waterways and in marked channels. When permissible it is blissfully simple compared to mooring, but lying at anchor can have its drawbacks and problems.

> NEVER LEAVE A BOAT UNATTENDED IF IT IS LYING ON A SINGLE ANCHOR OR MUDWEIGHT.

Someone must stay on board as 'anchor watch'. (Any 'resident' boats you see apparently lying at anchor unmanned are probably on a mooring, which is safe.)

Prepare by getting the anchor or mudweight secured to the anchor chain or the bow rope, and just before coming up hang it just over the bow (if there is a roller), or below the fairlead.

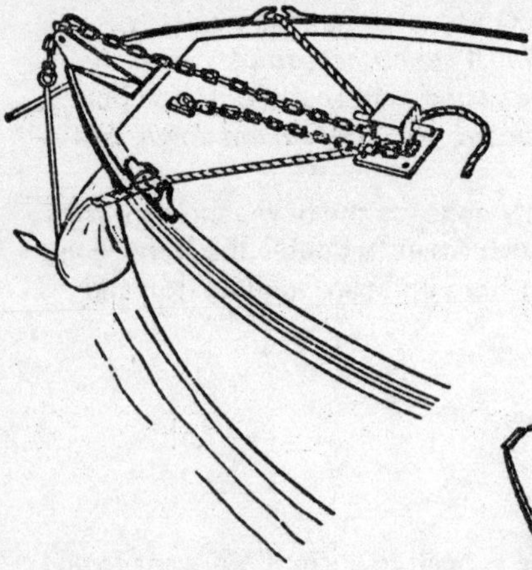

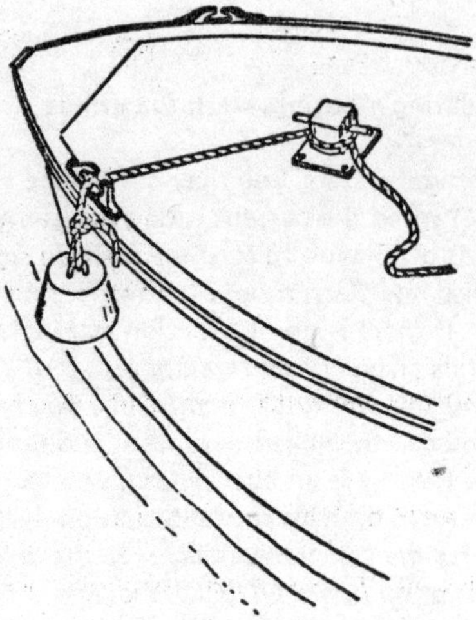

MAKE SURE THE ANCHOR CANNOT DROP AND IS NOT LET GO BEFORE YOU ARE READY. Basically, as for mooring against the bank, you come up head to current and/or wind. But you can see the *exact direction of approach from the way boats already at anchor or on a mooring buoy are lying:*

Unless they are anchored at bow and stern (*), in which case they will not indicate the direction of approach, *all these boats – and yours –*

will swing on the wind or tide; and for various reasons, they may not all swing together. *So when coming in to drop anchor, you have to envisage a pattern of circles on the water, and to make sure that your circle will clear the other boats, the bank and any other fixed object or hazard.*

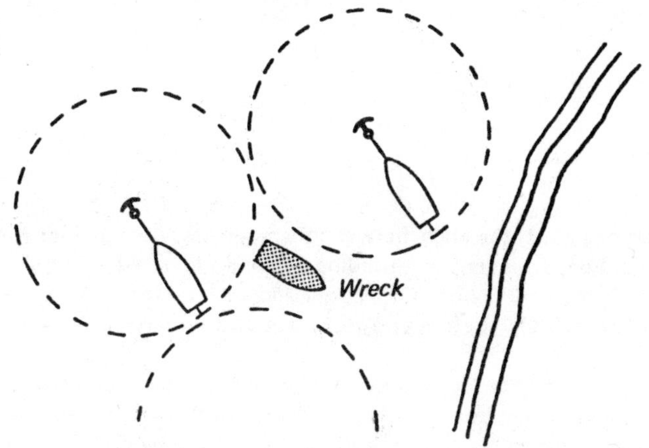

Having chosen the spot to drop the anchor and fixed it in your mind's eye, turn onto the approach line well downwind/down-current of this point and let the boat 'carry' up to it, adjusting if needs be by going slow ahead or astern. *When the boat is stationary relative to the LAND, drop the anchor.* Keep hands clear of the rope or chain. You will know when the anchor or mudweight reaches the bottom. *Let out about half as much rope or chain again, and then secure it.* With rope, just let out enough to give a comfortable angle, as it will not help to hold you. With chain, the more you let out (within reason) the more secure you will be – but the larger your swinging circle and the greater the labour of getting it up again.

Dragging your anchor

The danger of lying at anchor is 'dragging', i.e. the pressures on your boat from wind and current are so strong that the anchor or mud-weight is pulled along the bottom and you drift – eventually into danger. If you are using a chain, dragging produces a quite characteristic – and very alarming – clunking noise and juddering. With a rope and a muddy bottom however there is no such warning.

So you choose a *'transit'* and get someone to watch it until you are sure the anchor is holding and then to check it at fairly short intervals.

Pick two prominent fixed objects on the bank (or maybe buoys) to

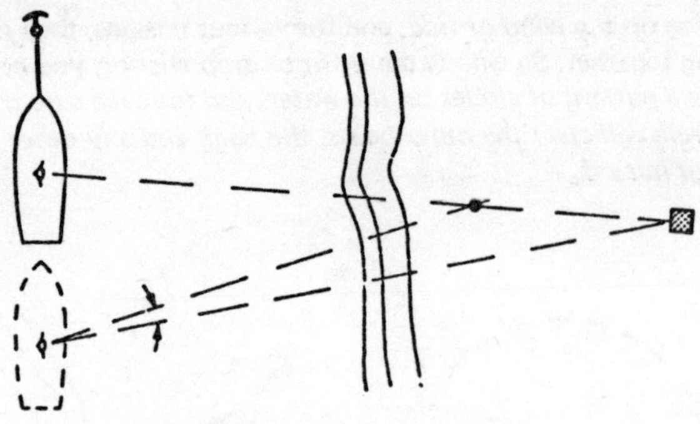

one side of you. If the angle between them remains the same, or if they remain in line, your anchor is holding. If the angle between them changes or they come out of line, your anchor is probably dragging.

But double-check before you get worried, as you may just be swinging.

Boats at anchor at night show a *single white light* all round at the highest point on the boat, the *'riding light'*, but this is often not done on inland waters where most navigation takes place by day.

Weighing anchor

To get the anchor or mudweight up, simply pull in the rope or chain, helping if needs be by going slow ahead. When you are over the anchor, i.e. the rope or chain is vertical, simply pull it up as quickly as you can and once it is clear of the water, go slow ahead.

If the anchor sticks, *'break it out'* by pulling in the rope as far as you can, securing it, and then going hard ahead, or if necessary backwards and forwards, until it comes clear.

Be careful not to let the anchor or mudweight swing or be forced against the side of the boat. The anchor/mudweight and chain/rope may be very dirty. Be prepared for this. Get as much mud, etc. as you can off while the anchor is still over the side. When you have cleaned and recovered it, sluice the foredeck with plenty of water.

7 Safety and comfort on board

Even on inland waters in summer, grown men can get cold, wet and exhausted surprisingly quickly; and even on fine days the evening 'moorings race' produces its stresses and hazards. So being well-organised adds to safety as well as to enjoyment. Use the independence your boat gives you – after all it was to get away from pressures that you came on a boating holiday.

Refuelling, watering and 'pumping out'

Modern diesel-engined motorcruisers carry enough fuel for at least a week of normal inland water cruising. Water is more of a problem; even if you are careful with it, a crew can get though as much as the boat can carry in a day or two. And 'pumping out' of the toilet can become the most pressing problem of all.

If you are cruising every day:

1 Do the checks called for in the Instruction Book or Skipper's Manual *each morning before you start off.*

2 Unless you are quite sure you have enough water in the tank and toilet capacity to last till the next day, *call in at the FIRST fuel station you pass. Don't* leave it till the evening.

If you are staying in the same place for a day or two, *do your checks daily (and run the engine, see below), and know where the nearest fuel and water* can be found.

TAKE CARE WHEN REFUELLING – DON'T OVERFILL AND DON'T SMOKE.

Petrol is dangerous if it gets in the bilges or anywhere else it should not be. If you have the least suspicion that petrol may have leaked or spilled over, *stop smoking, turn off the gas, have everyone wearing buoyancy aids and stop the engine as soon as possible.* Don't start or restart the engine. If it is a hire-boat get it checked by an expert; *if it is your own, pump out and flush the bilges (see below)* and, of course deal with any leak.

After filling up with petrol, and always before starting the engine, it is wise to check that there is no smell of petrol in the engine compartment or bilges, let the engine run for a few minutes before casting off and apply the precautions mentioned above for a short while.

Diesel fuel is less dangerous (although it can both burn and explode), but it is unpleasant stuff. It smells, ruins food, stains clothes and may affect the skin. Clean out the bilges (see below) if diesel fuel leaks or is spilt. If you are subject to 'diesel rash', use a good barrier cream before contact and/or a soothing hand cream afterwards; and change and wash your clothes if they have any traces of diesel on them.

Batteries

Flat batteries are the commonest cause of 'breakdown' in hire-boats, and getting them changed or charged can easily lose you a day. On days when you cruise for an hour or more there should be no problem. But 36 hours or more without charging is more than most batteries will stand. *Run the engine for a time* (see Instruction Book or Skipper's Manual) *on any day you stay on moorings or at anchor.*

Gas

Most boats carry a spare gas cylinder ('bottle') and you can make the changeover yourself if needs be. *Having changed a bottle make sure that you replace the empty next time you call at a boatyard or suitable shop.*

Note: the Calor Gas valve has a left-hand thread and requires a special spanner. Camping Gaz has a right-hand thread and requires no tools. Make sure you do not pull the rubber tube away from the valve when fitting.

This gas is heavier than air. If it leaks or a tap is left on, it will sink into the bilges and can form *an explosive gas-air mixture which is easily ignited.* Quite apart from this risk, once in the bilges it is very difficult to get out.

Always have the match or lighter burning BEFORE you turn the gas on.

Always keep an eye on a low flame and make sure it is sheltered from wind or draughts.

(On most cookers, you turn the tap *beyond* the full on position to get a low flame; this is much safer than turning it back towards **off.**)

Turn the gas off AT THE CYLINDER when not in use, unless the cylinder is serving any gas appliances which run constantly.

Check refrigerators, water-heaters, heating, etc., before leaving the boat or going to sleep, and on returning or first thing in the morning.

IF YOU SMELL A GAS LEAK, TREAT IT SERIOUSLY:

Turn off ALL supplies at the cylinder(s).

Turn off the electric master switch.

Do not start the engine.

Open up all hatches, windows, sliding roof, etc.

Make sure everyone is wearing buoyancy aids.

Get everyone into the open wheelhouse/cockpit or on deck.

Get everyone ashore and go or telephone for help.

Bilges

The bottom of the inside of the boat is called the bilges, and some water collects there in all boats.

Check your bilges daily, even if you have an automatic bilgepump. *If the amount of water in the bilges increases* (or the automatic pump is working overtime) *there may be a leak.* Try to locate it; get in touch with a boatyard if necessary. On hire-boats *don't* attempt to repair a leak or even tighten up the stern gland yourself – get help.

The bilges may get contaminated with petrol, diesel fuel, gas, oil or fluids from the toilet. *If it's gas, take action as above.* In any case it is best to go to a boatyard or fuel station where possible. The procedure is:

Pump the bilges dry.
Run in water (but don't sink the boat!).
Add detergent and let it stand.
Pump dry.

Rinse with more water and pump dry.
Repeat as necessary.

If you use an automatic or other electric bilgepump, run the engine to stop the batteries going flat.

Ventilation

Living-space in a boat is much smaller than at home. *Remember that all gas appliances use oxygen;* this includes refrigerators, water-heaters, central heating and – easiest to forget about – catalytic (flameless) heaters. *So make sure you always have a window, ventilator or hatch a bit open when there is a gas flame burning. NEVER stop up ventilation louvres, grilles, etc.*

Central heating/heaters

Take special care when using heaters; fire can spread very quickly in a small, confined space.

Don't hang wet clothes, teacloths, etc., actually over heaters or let then come in direct contact. Make sure any inflammable material near the heater is not getting too hot.

Always check that all grilles, louvres, etc., of heaters are clear and that air can flow freely through and round them.

It is best to turn heaters off before going to bed, but if you do leave a heater or the central heating on, *double-check that the cabin is ventilated, that all inflammable materials are well clear of heaters, and that bedding cannot fall or be pushed onto hot surfaces or flames.*

Keeping warm and dry

In bad weather, even healthy young adults get cold, wet and exhausted working the boat – children and older people much more so. When you are cold and exhausted, your concentration and judgement goes and you may take stupid risks, especially to get onto a mooring quickly.

This is something that takes people who are not used to boats (or for that matter mountains) completely by surprise. So take a good lightweight waterproof 'top', preferably with a hood, and plenty of sweaters with you, and put them on in good time. Keep your head dry and have a spare towel to wrap round your neck. If you get wet, change your clothes as soon as you can get below.

Shoes

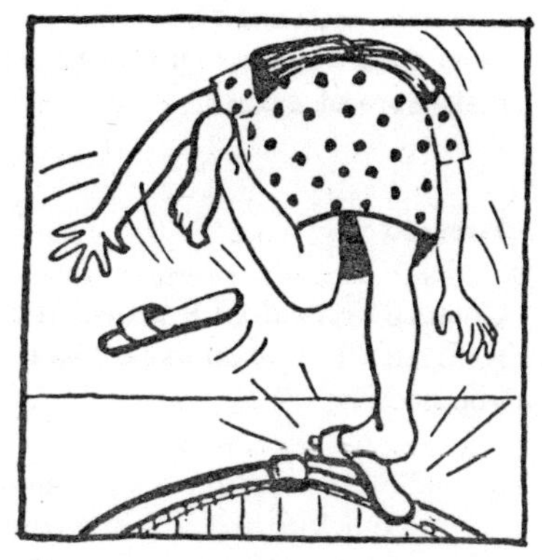

Sailing shoes with non-slip soles are best, but whatever you wear just check whether they hold on the various surfaces on your boat, *wet as well as dry.* Some combinations of sole-pattern and surface can be – literally – lethal.

Don't wear flip-flops or other kinds of sandal which are not firmly strapped. They may catch on an edge, trip you and send you headfirst overboard.

Don't go barefoot when you are doing something on board. You are very likely to hurt your foot by treading on a protrusion or dropping something on it, and this may distract you and make you let go of a rope or make a stupid mistake.

If the banks or the ground beyond them are likely to be muddy, keep an old pair of shoes or sea-boots (ankle-length rubber boots) in the cockpit and use these just for mooring, etc. *But NEVER wear knee or thigh boots on board*; if you fall in, they will fill with water and drag you down.

Catering

Having read this far you will begin to see why the catering on board affects safety as well as enjoyment. Always keep at least one day's food and drink in hand and *24 hours' reserve* – 'hard rations' – on top of that. Then you can always sit tight for a day if the weather turns foul, and shopping or eating and drinking ashore becomes a pleasure you can take when you wish and not a desperate necessity.

Moorings round pubs and shops are often crowded in season, and a good deal of racing and battling for places goes on. This is stressful at the best of times, and even if you are too wise to take risks to get a

place or get ashore, others may.

A well-victualled boat makes you independent of all this. But if you must moor for the night by a particular pub, get there in good time and make sure of a place.

First aid

Unless a first-aid kit is provided on the boat, take one with you. There is no need to buy an expensive ready-made-up kit; for inland waters all you need is:

1 Soluble asprin (or equivalent), anti-histamine cream (and maybe a quick-acting anti-bite spray), a good antiseptic cream, a spray or lotion for burns (ask your doctor – no two agree about this), eye lotion, liquid disinfectant (suitable for use on the person), insect deterrent spray and tissues.
2 Assorted plasters (take plenty), cotton wool or gauze swabs, bandages, sticking plaster, triangular bandage (to make a sling), crepe bandage.
3 Scissors, forceps, safety-pins, eyebath, 2p piece for telephone.

Make sure you have an adequate supply of any prescription medicines you normally take.

It will usually be easy to get a doctor, or to obtain other skilled help, so you need, and normally should, do no more than you would at home. But it is important to keep anyone who is hurt warm and comfortable, and to reassure them that a doctor or other trained help will come quickly.

If you have anyone on board likely to need a doctor, e.g. an elderly person, an epileptic, etc., *don't moor* in places inaccessible by road.

It is an advantage to have someone on board trained in resuscitation ('kiss of life' etc.). Effective use of these methods really needs a few hours personal instruction, but the standard diagrams (see Chapter 8) will serve as a reminder.

8 Safety precautions and emergency drills

Use of buoyancy aids

Even a strong swimmer may be drowned if he falls into the water unexpectedly. He may hit his head as he falls, faint through shock from the cold water, be caught in weed or mud, or if the tide is strong, be swept away.

There is always a risk of falling overboard and this is much higher when there is no rail or parapet above waist level to prevent you. *The roof, the foredeck, some aft cockpits and most of all the narrow side-decks of motorcruisers are all dangerspots.*

There is a risk of falling in when stepping on board or ashore, especially until you realise that the boat moves when you step on or off it! And falling between bank and boat is very dangerous because of the likelihood of being knocked out, crushed or held under.

Remember – and make sure your children realise – that it is just as easy to fall in from the bank as from the boat, and the water is just as cold and wet.

Even on the gentlest of inland waters a number of people are drowned every year. If you want to prevent you and yours becoming a statistic the rule is:

CHILDREN WEAR BUOYANCY AIDS:

When the boat is under way, wherever they are in the boat.
When on moorings or at anchor unless they are safely inside the boat and cannot get out.
When they are playing on or near the bank.

EVERYONE WEARS BUOYANCY AIDS:

When they go on deck or ashore to carry out a manoeuvre.
If they are non-swimmers or have a heart condition. (Such adults should follow the rules for children.)

To be effective buoyancy aids must be:

The right size
Correctly worn, i.e. tied tightly and securely

Otherwise they merely give an illusion of safety.

Wrong *Right*

Avoiding falling overboard

There are as many ways of falling in as there are boats. The best way to avoid them is to *move about the boat carefully and deliberately, wearing proper sailing shoes, and to keep a hand on something firm whenever you can. Be doubly careful when shoes and/or surfaces are wet.*

Skippers can greatly reduce the risk of a crewman falling overboard by *preparing for a manoeuvre in good time* and getting everyone briefed, organised and in the right place before things start happening.

But there are certain particularly common ways of falling overboard or causing someone else to, and all of them can be avoided:

1 Hold the boat in (or get someone else to) when going aboard or ashore.

2 *Never* get into or out of the dinghy, or remain in the dinghy, when the boat is under way.

3 *Don't* lean over the side to pick something up; use the boathook, etc., and get someone to hold your legs down.

4 *Don't* leave loose objects lying about on deck.

5 Coil ropes down neatly; or stow them in a locker.

6 *Don't* change course suddenly or start a manoeuvre without warning the crew.

7 Always secure the end of a rope you are going to pull on.

8 Keep your weight well inside the boat when using the boathook or heaving on a rope.

9 If you must fend, do it with *your feet not your hands* (see below). *NEVER fend with any part of your body when boats are moving. NEVER risk getting crushed.*

But sooner or later you will find a new way, so *wear your buoyancy aid.*

Bridges and high walls

People get swept overboard and/or severely crushed if they are caught between the deck or roof and a bridge or the side of a high wall. *Before passing under a bridge get everyone off the deck and account for everyone,* even if you think there is plenty of room.

When approaching a wall, get everyone inside the boat except those you need for fending or on the ropes, and *make a direct check that these crewmen are correctly positioned.*

Mooring and fending (see also Chapter 6)

Mooring and leaving moorings ('slipping') are the manoeuvres which carry the highest risk of injury, falling in or damage to the boat. *Plan carefully, take your time and DON'T go in too fast.*

Get fenders out and positioned, ropes ready and bow- and stern-men in position *in good time*. If possible cruise slowly past the mooring and let everyone have a look at it before turning and going in.

When fending is necessary, the only safe and effective position for fending is sitting facing outwards on the edge of the deck with your *legs out, toes up and knees slightly bent.* You can then apply your full shove in a controlled way and without risk of injury, *but never risk getting crushed.*

Remember you can fall in off the bank too. Keep your position and your weight away from the edge and make sure you have a firm foothold.

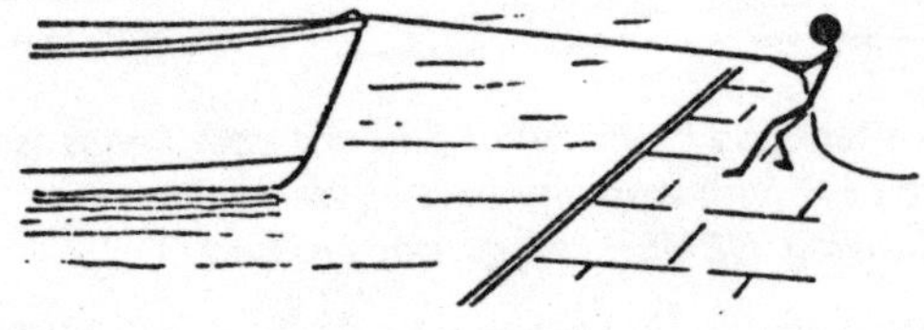

Discourage people from jumping ashore, and in particular *don't* ask anyone to jump further than he thinks he can. *Never* let children jump. If the rope snags, anyone jumping will fall between boat and bank. *It is up to you to bring the boat in close enough and slowly enough.*

If you are mooring up single or short-handed, have everything in position first. Lay the ropes so that you can pick them up from the helm position and step ashore with them. *Don't* head the boat in and then make a wild rush for the bows.

Casting off

Warn everyone before casting off. *Don't* let your crew or any helper ashore cast you off until you tell them to, even if there is no wind or current.

Whenever possible, *'double' ropes* – and/or take the final hold with the boathook – to avoid leaving someone ashore until the last moment.

Explain what you intend to do – at least it will serve to clear your own mind!

Man overboard

Shout 'Man overboard' loudly – for other boats and anyone on the bank to hear.

Throw a lifebelt – but make sure you don't hit the person in the water with it! Instruct one of your crew to keep the person in the water in view all the time. *Turn the boat back at once, claiming priority over all other traffic.* A sharp U-turn will also serve to reduce your speed.

Approach slowly the spot where you see the person or expect them to be. Allow for current. If you have lost sight of them give each of the crew a direction to look in until you have spotted them.

Don't let anyone else jump in unless the man in the water is going down or struggling. But it is worth putting a *strong swimmer wearing a buoyancy aid* in to comfort and help a child or elderly person; if you can put him in on a bowline at the end of a mooring rope or such, so much the better. If you are not ready to pick him/them up, pass down something that floats, e.g. an oar, for them to cling to, but make sure you *don't* hit them with it.

Don't run or drift over the person in the water. Bring the boat up head to wind just downwind of him. Current does not matter because the boat and the man in the water are both moving with it, unless, of course, you are drifting into danger. *Pass them a line,* preferably with a large loop in the end (bowline) that can be put under his or her arms. *They are now safe.*

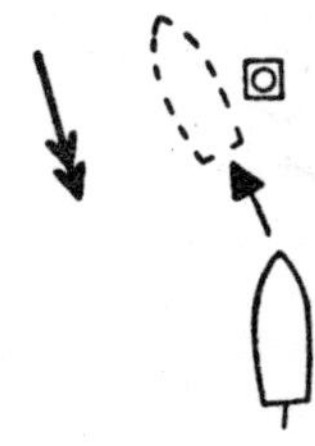

PUT GEAR IN NEUTRAL BEFORE TRYING TO GET THEM ABOARD. Propellors can cause serious injury. *Lift them on board, usually over the stern.* Get as many people as you can to help; they will be heavier than you expect. Get any water out of their lungs.

Bring your boat under control again. Get the victim below and stripped. Wrap them up warmly, treat for shock and deal with any minor injuries. They should see a doctor as soon as possible, particularly in polluted waters.

Action by man in water

If you yourself fall into the water, then remember to:

Shout as you fall, in case no-one sees you.
Trust your buoyancy aid; turn on your back and relax.
If you can reach a lifebelt or any other floating object, cling to it. This makes you easier to spot as well as supporting you.
In a narrow waterway make for the bank; otherwise stay where you are until it is obvious that your boat is not going to turn back or has done so and failed to spot you.

Breakdowns

If your boat breaks down:

1 On a river or canal, make for the bank and get a rope ashore. Then moor up safely, sort yourself out and, if possible, send someone to telephone for help – or hail another boat.

2 On a broad, lake, or in a narrow waterway if you are in danger, drop your anchor or mudweight, turning your head to current or wind first if you can. This will stop you drifting into danger. If you require help, hail a passing boat. If you hail for a tow, *offer them your rope.* This is for reasons of safety as well as courtesy.
If you require help and are stuck in the middle of a large expanse of water with no way of reaching the banks, hoist the International Code flag V (red X on white). Don't fire a flare unless you are in danger.

Going aground

As soon as you suspect you may be aground, *go astern.* Get everyone to the stern so that the bow rises. Keep going astern. Get your crew to move their weight from side to side to rock the boat.

If all this fails, try *pushing with the boathook or oar* on the bank or on the bottom, while keeping the other actions going.

If you are still stuck, keep going hard astern until you have *dropped an anchor or mudweight over the stern,* being very careful that the rope does not foul the propellor. This will stop you drifting harder on.

If you have no dinghy, there is little you can do but hail for a tow or (in tidal waters) wait for the tide to rise.

If you have a *dinghy*, use it to take your stern rope, with an anchor or mudweight on the end, as far as it will go away from the bank or shoal and drop it. Then organise your crew to heave on this rope while going hard astern. Even if the anchor drags, you will often get off in two or three attempts.

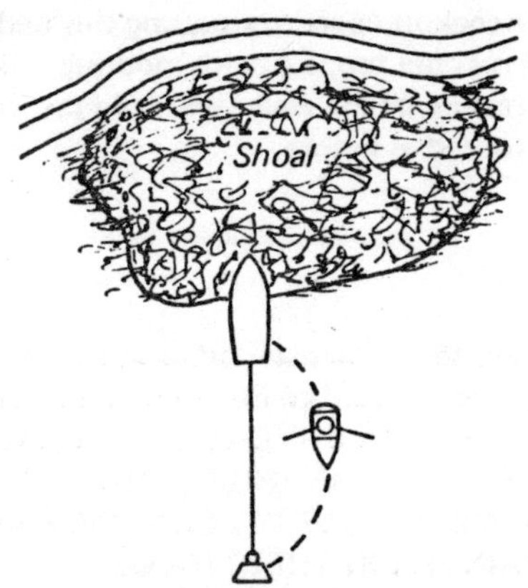

On narrow waterways, it is, of course, even better to get the dinghy to take the rope to a fixed object in midstream or to the opposite bank. But if you do this, *mark the rope with a flag or handkerchiefs and get your dinghy crew to control traffic.* Have someone standing by with a knife to cut the rope if other craft or their crews are endangered.

Make sure your crew keep the rope taut as your boat comes free and put the gear in neutral as you come back over the anchor, otherwise you are almost certain to get the stern rope round your propellor.

Action if holed

The first signs that you have been holed below the waterline will probably be the bow looking lower than usual and a loss of speed and manoeuvrability. Then, or if you have heard or felt any impact, *check the bilges.* Make sure everyone is warned, on deck and that they have their buoyancy aids on. Also ensure that everyone has a clear escape route. If water is coming in, *put a person on the hand bilge pump* to back up the electric pump, and find out where the damage is.

If you are on a narrow waterway with soft banks, the safest thing to do is to *run the boat's bows up the bank.* Then get a rope ashore to keep it there, and post one of your crew to hail passing boats to slow down. Any damage that results from running up the bank is likely to be less than would be caused by taking in a lot of water.

If you are on open water or the bank is hard, high or canalised, *stop the boat.* Keep pumping. Try to plug the hole from inside, forcing the hull back into shape if needs be. Use bedding, etc. If this works, build it up so that the plug is wedged solid between the hull and some fixed object inside. Then pump dry and make *slowly* for the nearest mooring or boatyard, keeping an eye on the bilges.

If repair from the inside fails and you have a large sheet, e.g. a hood or cockpit cover, try passing this under the hull and lashing it tight across the top, e.g. with mooring ropes. The advantage of this is that the pressure of the water will hold the sheet hard against the hull. Then proceed as before.

Fire

Fire, sometimes started or accompanied by an explosion, is probably the greatest hazard to life both on inland waters and at sea. If fire breaks out, GET EVERYONE ON DECK WITH BUOYANCY AIDS ON, READY TO ABANDON SHIP. IF YOU HAVE A DINGHY, HAVE SOMEONE GET IT ALONGSIDE AND GET IN IT OR TAKE ITS PAINTER IN THEIR HAND.

If you locate the fire before it has developed, attack it with the hand extinguisher(s) and, of course, actuate any built-in fire-fighting systems. If the fire has 'developed', i.e. begun to spread, before you find its source or if the extinguishers fail to put it out, ABANDON SHIP IMMEDIATELY.

When in the water, *make sure you keep together.* If you have a dinghy, get one adult into it (over the stern) and then put the weakest members in it. *Don't* overload the dinghy so that it capsizes or sinks. Rearrange the rope(s) so that those who remain in the water can tie themselves on and be towed.

Rescue of other crews and boats

Your first responsibility is the safety of your own crew. *Don't attempt* a rescue operation that is beyond the capacity of your boat or your crew. Unless there is danger to life, tackle the problem deliberately so that you don't run into the same or other trouble yourself.

If there are people in the water, follow the "Man Overboard" drill above.

If a boat is broken down, take it in tow by picking up *its* bowrope, taking care not to get this round your propellor. On busy waterways, it is sometimes easier to tow alongside. *Always take the strain gently and make sure everything is clear before you go full ahead.*

If a boat is aground, *don't* go up to it to pick up its rope. If either boat has a dinghy, stay well clear and get the rope rowed across to you. If you have to get close to the stranded boat, *go in very slowly bow first* and *go hard astern* the moment you have its stern rope. Get the grounded boat to go astern. If you cannot pull it off by going astern, stay clear, but holding the rope, pass it from your bow to your stern turning as you do so, and then take the strain again and go full ahead.

If a boat is holed or on fire, your first responsibility is to get its crew safely on board.

If you go alongside, hold on with the boathook; *don't* put a rope on. Always approach the boat from the windward side and get clear as soon as you have its crew on board.

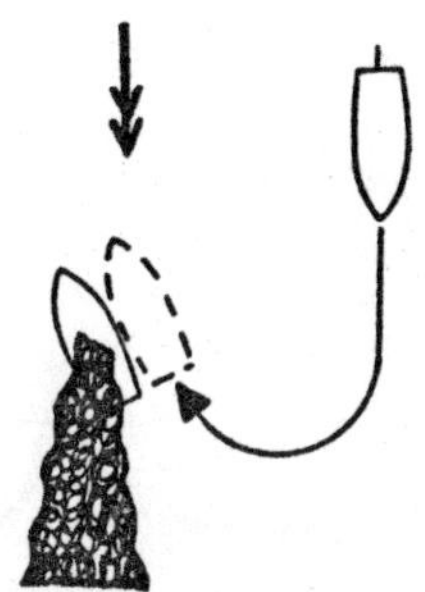

If the crew of a burning boat have buoyancy aids it will usually be much safer for all to recover them from the water.

When towing a boat that is holed or *has* been on fire, always have a crew member armed with a sharp knife watching it and ready to cut the rope.

Mouth-to-mouth resuscitation

It is to be hoped that you never have to revive one of your crew; but if you have to the following method of artificial respiration (reproduced by kind permission of the British Safety Council) should be started *as soon as possible.*

1 *Position of head* Tilt victim's head as shown below to open the airway. At this point the airway can be cleared with the fingers (of any obstruction).

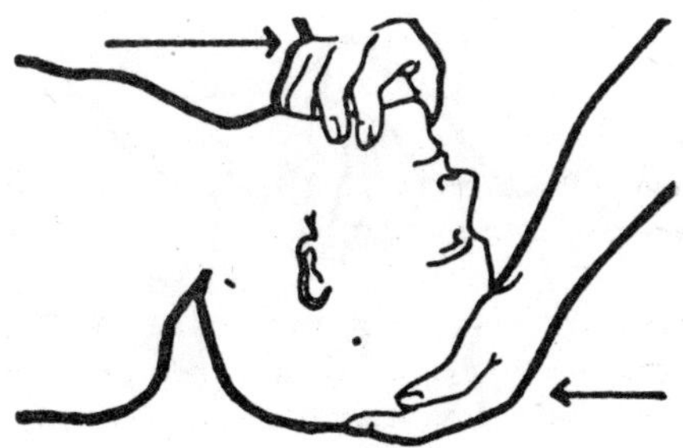

2 *For mouth-to-nose* Close the victim's mouth with thumb. Place your mouth over victim's nose (shaded area) and blow. Remove your mouth, and look for movement of chest. If this does not occur, check head position and try again. If unsuccessful change to mouth-to-mouth.

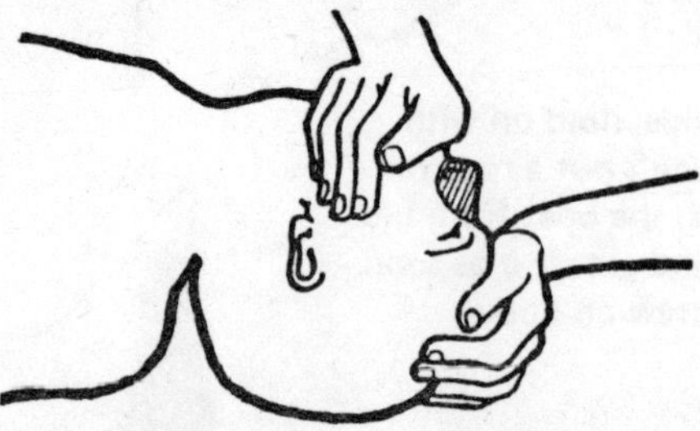

3 *Mouth-to-mouth* Close victim's nose by pinching nostrils. Place your mouth over the victim's mouth (shaded area) and blow.

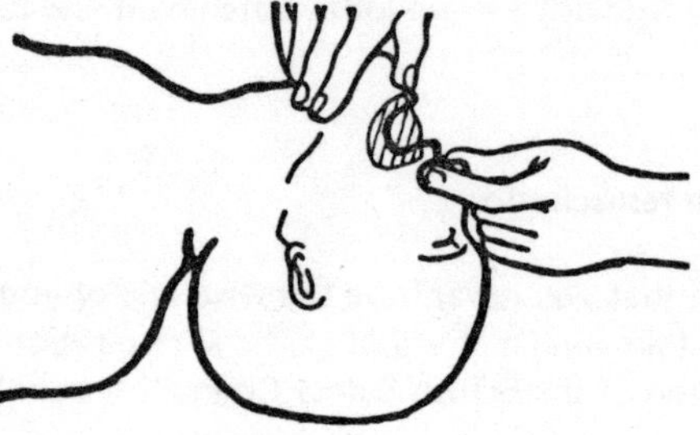

4 *Mouth-to-nose/mouth-to-mouth* Repeat at least 10 times a minute. Below is the position of the rescuer and victim in mouth to nose resuscitation.

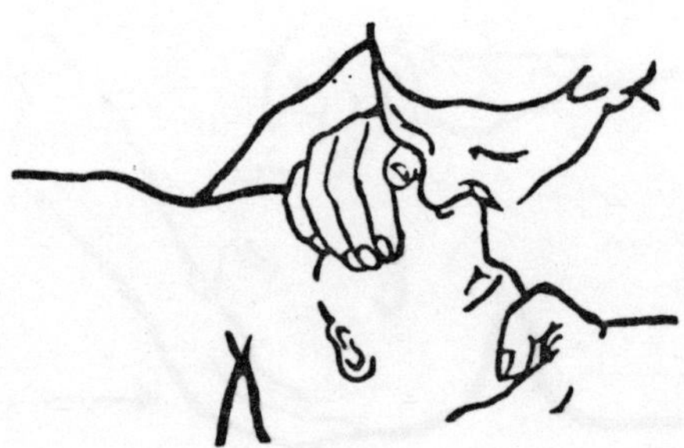

5 *For infants and small children* Cover both nose and mouth (shaded area). Smaller puffs are required; these should be repeated at least 20 times per minute.

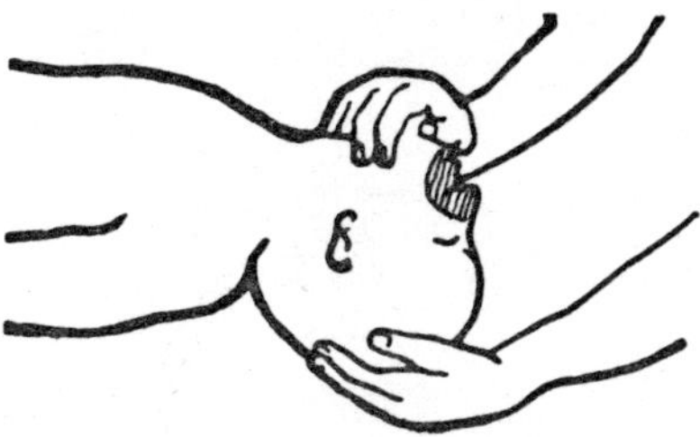

These hints are no substitute for a thorough knowledge of First Aid. This may be obtained by attending a course of instruction at your local First Aid organisation or branch of the Royal Life Saving Society.

9 Dinghies

A dinghy will add greatly to your enjoyment, and even more to your children's. It can also be very useful in an emergency. But perhaps its greatest advantage is that it allows you to moor or anchor a little way off the most crowded moorings and still get to the shops or pub easily.

If you hire a motorcruiser, you will often be able to hire a dinghy with it.

Safety rules

1. CHILDREN AND NON-SWIMMERS SHOULD ALWAYS WEAR BUOYANCY AIDS IN DINGHIES.
2. NEVER GET INTO OR OUT OF OR REMAIN IN A DINGHY BEING TOWED BY A MOVING BOAT.
3. If you want to put someone off in the dinghy or pick them up from it without mooring or anchoring, pull clear of the main traffic stream and bring your boat to rest.

Watermanship

Watermanship may be described as the art of not upsetting dinghies, and particularly of getting into and out of them without drama.

Always remember:

1 *Bring the dinghy ALONGSIDE the bank or boat – don't* get in or out over the ends.

2 *Make sure the dinghy is firmly tied up or held* – otherwise it will shoot away as soon as you step in or out of it.

3 *Always step into the bottom of the dinghy near the middle.*

4 *Don't step onto a seat* – your weight applied high up will tip the dinghy.

5 *Never jump into a dinghy – and don't let children!*

6 *Get in one at a time and sit down* – those already in use their weight to keep the dinghy level while the next one moves.

7 If you want to change places, *only one person moves at a time. Don't cast off until you are ready.*

Follow the same rules when getting out. *To get into a dinghy from the water, pull yourself over the stern.* If you are inside the dinghy helping, *don't* get too much weight at the stern. Always have a baler and a sponge (foam offcut) handy, and get rid of water as soon as it gets in. Tie the baler to the dinghy with a bit of cord long enough to allow you to use it freely.

Towing

Most dinghies will tow easily on a single rope. *Either* have the rope just

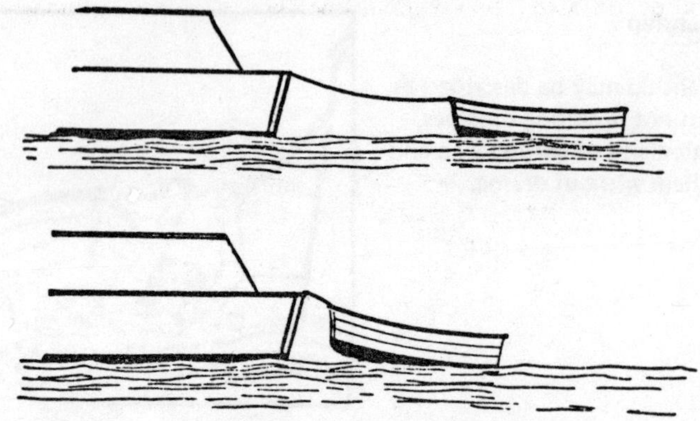

long enough to stop the dinghy bumping whenever you slow down or change direction, *or* have the dinghy right up short.

Make sure the dinghy and boat are well fended.

If the dinghy swings from side to side (some sailing dinghies do), put a double rope on it. *Don't* forget your dinghy when coming in to moor. They make good fenders, but expensive ones!

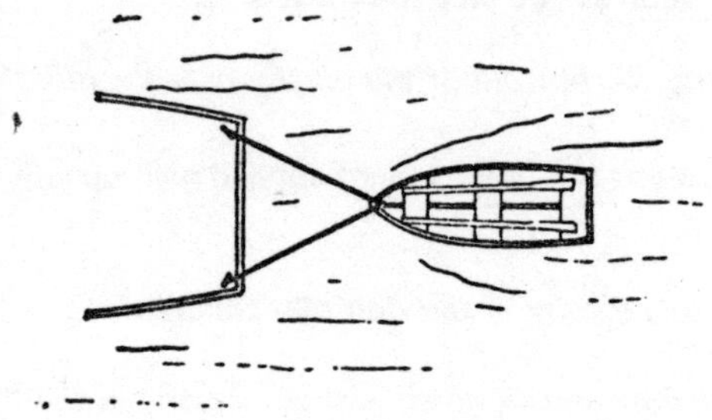

Rowing

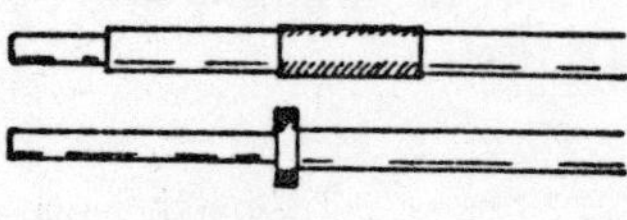

Pin-type rowlocks, which hold the oar securely, are very rare nowadays, especially on light dinghies. With normal rowlocks, *you will probably lose the oar if you let go of it, even if the oar has a collar on it.*

Always secure the rowlocks, and it is no bad idea to secure the oars with a bit of cord tied round them just below the handle and round the seat:

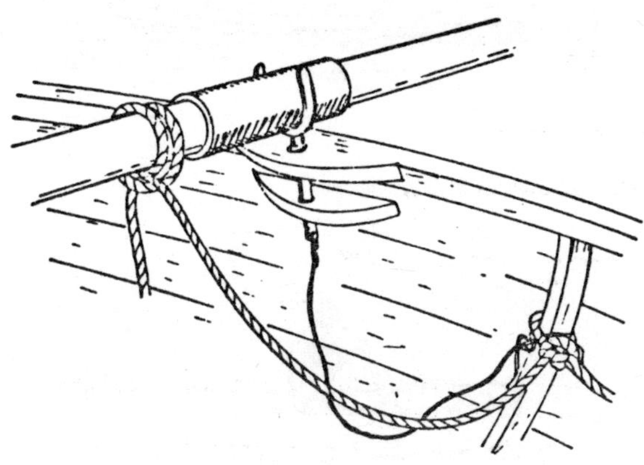

Make sure the oars are well stowed fully within the dinghy, and preferably lashed, before leaving the dinghy. Dismount the rowlocks so that they hang down inside the boat.

A dinghy is not a racing skiff or eight. Row with short strokes, the blade of the oar moving in an oval. Whether or not you 'feather', i.e. turn the blade flat while it is moving through the air, make sure the blade is facing slightly downwards in the water, or you will 'catch a crab'.

To steady the boat when you are not rowing, hold the oars square to the boat with the blades flat on the water.

The rower sits facing the stern and so needs to be guided. *Tell him which of HIS hands to pull with – this is the same as YOUR hand on the side you want to boat to go. To go astern* the rower *pushes* one or both oars through the water, reversing the normal cycle. As with a motorboat, this is also how you brake.

To *turn round* the rower *pushes* with one oar and *pulls* with the other at the same time.

If you are guiding him alongside or up to the stern of a boat, the orders for slowing down and reversing are 'Back left' (his hand), 'Back right' or 'Back her down' (both).

If you are rowing on your own, turn your head frequently to see where you are going and that all is clear.

If you hear a hail 'Ahead, dinghy' or such, it means that you are about to obstruct another boat. *Push on both oars to stop, and look round.*

Start of stroke: blades just in water

End of stroke

Drop hands to clear blades from water

Blades above water ready for next stroke

Steadying boat with blades flat on water, handles held

Turning, i.e. 'pull right, back left' (or vice versa)

Sailing dinghies

Before taking a sailing dinghy in tow, make sure all the bits and pieces are securely stowed and preferably lashed down. Raise or lift out the centreboard and dismount the rudder. On convertible dinghies, lower or dismount the mast.

ALWAYS WEAR A BUOYANCY AID or LIFEJACKET, even if you can swim. (See note, page 14.)

Rubber dinghies

Rubber dinghies are ideal for children because they are light to handle, stable and buoyant, and can be taken round in the boot or on the roof-rack of a car.

You can pay anything from £15 to £150 or more for an 8-ft rubber dinghy. The more expensive ones are fully seaworthy – in fact they are used as liferafts by small seagoing yachts. *Many of the cheaper ones are toys, suitable for use only in paddling pools or other places where it is physically impossible for children to get out of their depth: they are NOT suitable for use with motorcruisers, even on sheltered inland waters.*

Outboard motors (for dinghies)

Don't buy or hire a larger or more complicated outboard than you need. Lightness, handiness and simplicity are usually more important than performance.

Always secure the outboard by a cord when there is any possibility of its falling in the water, especially when transferring it between cruiser and dinghy – and all the time it is in the dinghy, whether mounted or not. Remember, also, the following:

1 *Study the instructions carefully and follow them exactly.*
2 *Stop the engine by turning the fuel tap off and running the carburettor dry.*
3 *Then screw down the fuel tank vent.*
4 *Recheck the fuel tap vent before handling.*
5 Keep the starter toggle in a safe place.
6 Always carry a spare shear pin (and in some motors, propellor pin). The shear pin is designed to break if the propellor strikes a solid object or gets entangled with ropes, plastic bags, etc., thus protecting the motor. Always refer to the outboard motor instruction book.)

If the fuel tank is on the motor, *mount the motor on the dinghy to fill it so* that any petrol or 'petroil' spilt falls into the water. It may seem elementary to say DON'T SMOKE WHILE YOU ARE DOING THIS, but some nasty accidents have happened from this very cause. Use a funnel and pour very carefully. Make sure you have the right mix. Larger motors usually have separate pressure tanks; it is best to fill these ashore; again NO SMOKING!

Starting an outboard is a knack. You need to give a sharp pull on the toggle rope while keeping control of your weight. Put your left hand (assuming you are right-handed) on a *safe* part of the motor, i.e. a part that does not go round, and push down and away from you as you pull the toggle rope with your right hand. Never start the engine without the propellor in the water.

After starting and frequently during running (especially in weedy waters), *check that water is coming from the water outlet.*

Always swing the outboard up out of the water (*after checking that the carburettor is dry, fuel tap off and fuel-tank vent closed*) when coming in to moor or beach and when preparing to tow the dinghy.

Summary

DO

Allow for wind and current/tide

Turn head to current and/or wind:
- When mooring/anchoring
- When in difficulty/danger

Check your mooring with boathook for:
- Obstructions
- Depth (tide)

Plan difficult passages carefully

Handle your boat on ropes in tight places

Keep in the channel:
- Away from sea — black to right
- Towards sea — red to right

Keep to the right

Keep well clear of boats you are overtaking

Give way to boats moving with current, sail, boats towing

Prepare for mooring/anchoring thoroughly and in good time

Double the mooring rope before casting off

Carry out daily checks and keep a margin of fuel, water and food in hand

Sniff for petrol after filling up and *before* starting engine

Light match *before* you turn the gas on

Turn gas off at cylinder when not in use

Take full precautions if you smell gas

Check that grilles, etc., of heaters are clear

Make sure children wear buoyancy aids on board, in dinghy or near water

Make sure non-swimmers wear buoyancy aids on deck and when mooring, etc.

Get everyone below for bridges

Make sure everyone knows man overboard and fire drills

Do's and Dont's

DON'T

Turn sharply when you are near the bank

Go hard astern on full lock or when changing lock

Turn upstream (up-tide) of a bridge or obstruction

Cross a waterway or start a manoeuvre unless the way is clear

Cut across the bows of a sailing boat

Come in to moor too fast

Come in to moor before your crew, ropes, etc., are ready

Let ropes trail in the water

Let your boat hang on its ropes

Cast off before the engine is warm and you are ready

Get too near a downwind shore

Make your crew jump gaps when mooring or casting off

Fend with your hands

Leave a boat unattended on a single anchor/mudweight

Start or restart engine if you smell petrol or gas

Have any gas device on without adequate ventilation – remember the fridge

Go barefoot, or wear flip-flops, clogs, knee or thighboots on board

Get or remain in the dinghy when it is being towed

Lean over the side to pick something up

Start a manoeuvre without warning crew

Jump into or out of a dinghy or step on the seat

Carry more than 12 people in a boat

Use any form of firearm (including airguns) from a boat

Spoil others' enjoyment by excessive noise, etc.

The Country Code

(Reproduced by kind permission of The Countryside Commission.)

The Country Code was written to help reduce or prevent the unintentional damage that occurs every year, particularly at public holidays. Too many visitors to the countryside are unfamiliar with its ways. They forget that a single careless act—a gate left open, a fence or hedge weakened, a dropped cigarette end—can mean a lot of extra work and expense for farmers, foresters and other country folk.

The Code is a series of ten reminders based on common sense—and common failings. So when in the country remember:

Guard against all risk of fire

Plantations, woodlands and heaths are highly inflammable: every year acres burn because of casually dropped matches, cigarette ends or pipe ash.

Fasten all gates

Even if you found them open. Animals can't be told to stay where they're put. A gate left open invites them to wander, a danger to themselves, to crops and to traffic.

Keep dogs under proper control

Farmers have good reason to regard visiting dogs as pests: in the country a civilised town dog can become a savage. Keep your dog on a lead wherever there is livestock about, also on country roads.

Keep to the paths across farm land

Crops can be ruined by people's feet. Remember that grass is a valuable crop too, sometimes the only one on the farm. Flattened corn or hay is very difficult to harvest.

Avoid damaging fences, hedges and walls

They are expensive items in the farm's economy; repairs are costly and use scarce labour. Keep to the recognised routes, using gates and stiles.

Leave no litter

All litter is unsightly, and some is dangerous as well. Take litter home for disposal; in the country it costs a lot to collect it.

Safeguard water supplies

Your chosen walk may well cross a catchment area for the water supply of millions. Avoid polluting it in any way. Never interfere with cattle troughs.

Protect wild life, wild plants and trees

Wild life is best observed, not collected. To pick or uproot flowers, carve trees and rocks, or disturb wild animals and birds, destroys other people's pleasure as well.

Go carefully on country roads

Country roads have special dangers, blind corners, high banks and hedges, slow-moving tractors and farm machinery or animals. Motorists should reduce their speed and take extra care; walkers should keep to the right, facing oncoming traffic.

Respect the life of the countryside

Set a good example and try to fit in with the life and work of the countryside. This way good relations are preserved, and those who follow it are not regarded as enemies.